Civic Education in the Elementary Grades

Civic Education in the Elementary Grades

Promoting Student Engagement in an Era of Accountability

Dana Mitra *and* **Stephanie C. Serriere**
Foreword *by* Meira Levinson

TEACHERS COLLEGE PRESS

TEACHERS COLLEGE | COLUMBIA UNIVERSITY
NEW YORK AND LONDON

Published by Teachers College Press, 1234 Amsterdam Avenue, New York, NY 10027

Excerpts from two articles from the National Council for the Social Studies' *Social Studies and the Young Learner* and *Theory and Research in Social Education* have been used with permission.

Library of Congress Cataloging-in-Publication Data

Mitra, Dana L.
    Civic education in the elementary grades : promoting student engagement in an era of
    accountability / Dana Mitra, Stephanie Serriere.
        pages cm
    Includes bibliographical references and index.
    ISBN 978-0-8077-5634-8 (pbk. : alk. paper)
    ISBN 978-0-8077-5636-2 (hardcover : alk. paper)
    ISBN 978-0-8077-7345-1 (ebook)
        1. Civics—Study and teaching (Elementary)—United States—Handbooks, manuals,
    etc. I. Serriere, Stephanie Cayot II. Title.
    LB1584.M64 2015
    372.83'044—dc23   2015025967

ISBN 978-0-8077-5634-8 (paper)
ISBN 978-0-8077-5636-2 (hardcover)
ISBN 978-0-8077-7345-1 (ebook)

Printed on acid-free paper
Manufactured in the United States of America

22 21 20 19 18 17 16 15   8 7 6 5 4 3 2 1

Contents

Foreword

Many people—including even many who profess a belief that "all children can learn" and that "every child deserves a great teacher"—focus on what children and teachers *cannot* do, *are not* doing, or *will not* do. By contrast, this is a book about what children, teachers, and school leaders *can* do and *are* doing. By diving deep into the extraordinary world of Dewey Elementary School, Dana Mitra and Stephanie Serriere demonstrate how young children—with support and guidance and also a strong dollop of adults-getting-out-of-the-way—are year-in and year-out developing knowledge, skills, habits, and identities as empowered citizens who can work collectively to solve important problems and to exercise leadership among other children and adults. By providing such a rich vision of what is possible, as well as clear accounts of the opportunities and challenges that members of the Dewey community faced, *Civic Education in the Elementary Grades: Promoting Student Engagement in an Era of Accountability* will ideally inspire others to re-imagine how primary school can help support young children's development and deployment of their civic capacities. Furthermore, this is an admirable work of civic engagement in its own right.

In service of this aim, let me offer two key insights I derived from reading *Civic Education in the Elementary Grades*, as well as two thoughts about how I think its rich accounts of practice may support educators' work moving forward in an era of both accountability and standardized curricular frameworks, such as the Common Core.

The first insight is that Mitra and Serriere show that there is no single right or best way of teaching civic engagement, just as there is no single best way to engage as a citizen at the local, national, or global level. Rather, students and educators alike can and should seek multiple pathways to collective civic action.

These pathways may be at different *levels* of engagement; Mitra and Serriere highlight how students and teachers at Dewey engage civically at the classroom, school, and community levels. Furthermore, the community level itself extends from city to state to globe, as students reach across town to a local homeless shelter, across the state to win awards for green practices, and across the world to fund a school library in Tanzania.

Students and educators may also undertake different *forms* of engagement. Civic engagement takes a stunning range of forms at Dewey, including service-learning, public speaking, democratic deliberation, direct engagement/activism, participatory action research, listening, volunteering, testifying, and protesting.

Children and adults also may address multiple *substantive issues,* and/or they may tackle the same issue from *multiple perspectives.* Environmentalism is a common substantive focus at Dewey, for example, but students tackle it from a variety of perspectives, including zero waste partnerships (see "In Their Own Words: Becoming a Zero-Waste School" by Principal Shannon), the Schoolyard Project (see Chapter 5, "Environmental Stewardship: Giving Teachers Reasons to Participate"), and peer awareness/consciousness-raising within the school (see Chapter 4, "Civic Zines in 5th Grade: Responses to the Call to 'Making a Difference'"). In addition to environmentalism, Dewey students and faculty are also engaged with issues of homelessness, animal welfare, standardized testing, school lunch options, the needs of service members abroad, and education in Africa, among other topics. It is an incredibly rich array of substantive concerns, tackled through multiple modes of engagement at many different levels.

This diversity of approaches illuminates how democratic participation requires a wide range of skills. As Principal Shannon teaches the "Salad Girls" (see Chapter 8, "Challenging District Policy Through Student Inquiry"), petitions and protests are often the last civic resort in a democracy, not the first. Conducting power analyses (who has the power to change the salads in the cafeteria?), collecting data (who wants different salads at lunchtime?), and both listening and talking to those in power (we understand you need to satisfy USDA guidelines; here's our idea for how to do so with beans instead of meat) are all essential skills. When deployed effectively, as the Salad Girls do, they can even (spoiler alert) obviate the need for more confrontational forms of action.

Perhaps equally important, this diversity of approaches recognizes that democratic *citizens* and *participants* require a wide array of means of engagement. If everyone is marching in lockstep—as teachers and students are so often expected to do in public schools these days—that's a good sign that one is in an authoritarian (or even tyrannical) environment, not a democratic one. Mitra and Serriere provide beautiful examples of ways in which the same overall format—such as Small School Advisories and All-School Assemblies—can be reshaped by students or teachers to fit their specific beliefs, needs, and even temperaments. Not all of us can—or should—be activists or organizers. But we can—and should—engage civically. Dewey Elementary School models how diverse individuals and collectives can do so in ways that build upon our various strengths and inclinations.

A second key insight from the book is that even very young children have the capacity to engage civically and to make the world a better place. Most civic education and youth civic engagement researchers and advocates focus on older children: those in middle school, older adolescents, and even young adults. These are crucial stages for long-term civic identity development. But Mitra and Serriere do an essential service in demonstrating that younger children also have the capacity to develop as empowered civic actors in the here-and-now, and that by doing so they can improve the world we currently live in, as well.

The number of examples of children responding positively to adult-led initiatives as well as initiating projects themselves is almost overwhelming. This book constitutes an existence proof that young children can eagerly and competently participate in and even lead collective action when they are supported in doing so. I look forward as years go on to reading other accounts of elementary school children transforming the world, thanks to the examples and inspiration provided in this book.

Two final thoughts. *Civic Education in the Elementary Grades* offers a suggestive range of evidence that high-quality civic engagement initiatives can enhance students' academic, social, and emotional engagement. Civic education proponents frequently make such claims, although we rarely have detailed evidence to support our intuitions, especially at the whole-school level. This book shows how Principal Shannon and her teachers accomplish this. It reveals the nitty-gritty of how experienced teachers can enable children who are immersed in meaningful civic work also to engage more deeply with mathematical problem-solving, peer collaboration, literacy and social studies learning, and development of empathy and mutual trust.

Finally, I think this is a go-to book for any elementary school educator, school leader, or teacher educator who is trying to figure out how to put the College, Career, and Civic Life (C3) Frameworks for Social Studies State Standards into practice. So many of the examples that Mitra and Serriere discuss show how the C3's inquiry arc works in practice to shape student learning. In virtually every chapter, we see students developing questions and planning inquiries (Dimension 1), applying disciplinary concepts and tools both within and beyond social studies (Dimension 2), evaluating sources and using evidence (Dimension 3), and communicating conclusions to multiple audiences and taking informed and effective action (Dimension 4). As one of the contributing writers for the *C3 Frameworks*, I find it hard to imagine a more inspiring or insightful resource into how inquiry learning can be woven into elementary school curriculum, culture, and practice.

—Meira Levinson

Acknowledgments

We first and foremost extend our appreciation to the teachers, administrators, staff, students, and parents of Dewey Elementary School. We continue to be inspired by your vision and dedication to kids, to the profession, and to the community.

We would like to thank Penn State's Children, Youth, and Family Consortium of The Pennsylvania State University and Penn State's College of Education for grants that supported this research.

We would like to express our gratitude to Meira Levinson for taking time during a busy year to write the foreword to the book.

We extend our sincere thanks to our Penn State students and colleagues who participated in data collection for this book: Kristina Brezicha, Christine Crain, Kelly Duncan, Ana Diaz Fernandez, David Fuentes, Mark Hlavacik, Kevin Hulburt, Roi Kawai, Amber Mallow, Elizabeth Manning, Eve Mayes, Jennifer Lane Myler, Karen McCoy, Mary Elizabeth Meier, Marcy Milholme, Rebecca Misangyi, Jon Niles, Kyle Martin O'Donnell, Katherine Reed, Elliott Rosenbloom, Michelle Salopek, and Angel Zheng.

Additionally, previous publications on Dewey informed chapters in this book, including writing and research by Ulrika Bergmark, Peter Buckland, Michael Burroughs, Kristina Brezicha, Jennifer Cody, Roi Kawai, Mark Kissling, Eve Mayes, Lorraine McGarry, Katherine Reed, Donnan Stoicovy, and Angel Zheng.

We would also like to thank Ana Diaz, Jennifer Lane Myler, Brian Huff, and Stephen Kotok for editorial assistance.

Thank you to Tamar London of London Wolfe Photography for taking our headshots for the back cover.

We would like to extend our love and gratitude to our families and friends who nurtured and encouraged us through this project, culminating in this book. Dana would especially like to extend love and gratitude to Todd. To our future leaders of the world, Kaden, Carson, and Audrey—we dedicate this book to you.

Civic Education in the Elementary Grades

CHAPTER 1

Civic Engagement in an Elementary Setting

At Dewey Elementary* 450 students file into a multipurpose room in a U-shape singing "This Land Is Your Land." At the center of the room, 22 1st-graders eagerly await their chance to make a presentation to the school's All-School Assembly. Run by 5th-graders, these weekly, schoolwide assemblies serve as a platform for students to present projects to the student body, create a sense of school community, and gain leadership experience.

When the students are settled, the 1st-graders make a presentation about Earth Day. The group ends by saying, "Every day can be Earth Day here at Dewey!"

Taking the microphone, a tall, 1st-grade girl asks, "But I am only one student; how can I help?"

The girl passes the microphone to the next speaker, a brunette girl in a floral skirt. She announces, "Our class made a plan, and you can also be that one student that helps."

As the 1st-graders pass the microphone down the line, they compute the number of paper towels their class alone used during the school year. The final number: 38,232 paper towels. A murmur ripples through the room.

The 1st-graders then begin to pile up the boxes of paper towels that represent the number of paper towels they use in an average school year. The hum in the room grows. Stacked two high, the boxes extend all the way to the end of the line of 1st-graders.

A tall boy announces that his class has committed to using only one paper towel per hand washing.

Another 1st-grader asks, "I am only one student; how can I help?" Inviting the audience to look at the stack of boxes, another student tells the school that they can save more than 120 boxes of paper towels during the school year.

"That is the equivalent of 477,900 paper towels a year," a girl announces. She passes the microphone to a classmate who exclaims, "By using only one paper towel to dry our hands, we could save more than 2,800 trees a year!"

One last 1st-grader takes the microphone. "Dewey Elementary, do you think that you could join us in using only one paper towel to dry your hands? This will save 2,800 trees!"

From that day, Dewey indeed reduced paper towel use significantly. Stickers made by this group of students remain affixed to every paper towel receptacle, asking

---

*All names in this book are pseudonyms, including teachers, students, principals, and other identifying organizations.

students and staff to "only use one." The school, led by the principal and several committees of students, has moved toward a goal of becoming a "waste-free school," which they met in 2015. Inquiry projects about the school's environmental footprint abound in the past 3 years based off this moment of civic engagement.

Dewey Elementary School teaches children how to make a difference. Dewey offers a laboratory for studying civic engagement, a rare example for elementary schools in an era of testing accountability (Boyle-Baise, Hsu, Johnson, Serriere, & Stewart, 2008). Part of the mission of American public schools is providing opportunities for civic engagement, including teaching how young people can participate and question public ideas in their schools and communities. In a time of narrowing educational goals and within the constraints of a culture of accountability, this book offers an active model of civic engagement that can begin in students' first experiences of schooling. It explores these questions: In what spaces can civic engagement be fostered in elementary schools, given a narrowing of focus in U.S. curriculum, especially at the elementary level? How can a civic engagement focus influence a school's vision, school activities, and outcomes for students?

Research suggests that children in the elementary grades should have opportunities to learn how to develop civic habits and skills that can lead to active participation in society (Hahn, 1998; Torney-Purta & Lopez, 2006). Even so, the majority of U.S. schools fail to provide an education for engaged citizenship (Kirshner, 2004; Larson, 2000), especially at the elementary level (Boyle-Baise et al., 2008).

In marked contrast to European nations, the United States lacks any formal policy to spur youth participation. Youth participation in European nations, the United Kingdom, Canada, and Australia has been reinforced by formal policies and national educational structures. Influenced by Articles 12 through 15 of the United Nations' Convention on the Rights of the Child (CRC), youth participation is defined as a series of rights, including access to information, expression of views, and freedom to form collective organizations (United Nations, 1989).

The CRC highlights the need to bolster the capacity of young people and adults to enable child participation and the need for strong standards and accountability to guide this process, and European policies have aligned with these goals. Although the democratic foundation of the United States rests on the idea that participation is a fundamental right of citizenship (Ochoa-Becker, Morton, Autry, Johnstad, & Merrill, 2001), many U.S. policies actually inhibit the voices of young people. For example, in Pennsylvania, it is illegal for young people under the age of 18 to serve on a voting decisionmaking board. With Somalia ratifying the treaty in 2015, the United States is soon to become the only nation in the world that has not ratified the CRC.

In today's era of academic accountability, schools are spending less time fostering democracy and civic engagement (Fitchett & Heafner, 2010), especially at the elementary level (VanFossen, 2005), than they have done in the past. Recent national policies may have opened a window of opportunity for refocusing on the civic learning as part of academic learning. The initial Common Core State Standards (CCSS) released in 2010 largely ignored civics and social studies, integrating these subjects into the English language arts standards. The Common Core document called the College, Career, and Civic Life (C3) framework offers an expanded vision of civic and social studies standards (National Council for the Social Studies [NCSS], 2013). Although social studies and civics remain untested in most states and therefore likely will be left untaught, the C3 framework provides modes of applying democratic processes and establishes a strong stance on inquiry, including the value of questioning, use of evidence, and taking informed action.

CIVIC ENGAGEMENT AS MAKING A DIFFERENCE

This book is based on the premise that civic engagement should remain at the heart of education in U.S. schools. We define the concept of civic engagement as a particular form of agency—a way in which young people take individual or collective action that works toward improving identified issues of concern in a classroom, school, or community. Such activities can show young people how to make a difference in both their own lives and the lives of others (Eccles & Gootman, 2002; Kirshner, O'Donoghue, & McLaughlin, 2005; Mitra, 2004; Mitra & Serriere, 2012).

Within and across classroom spaces, we frame civic engagement as ongoing, process-based, and dialogic, more than simply a "value of the week" approach or an emphasis on the "right" answer. Instead, we view civic engagement as purposive and critical—a way to encourage young people to examine their environment, to notice and question injustices, and to take action to make things better. Students can learn to participate in their community and also to take responsibility to push for changes when they observe injustices. Students can develop a growing awareness of the needs of others and social responsibility. Students become aware of injustices, and they can seek civically responsible roles in which they consider how to take action.

Such a critical focus on making a difference pushes against the individualistic tendencies of civic educational practices. In a critical construction, civic engagement includes an examination of power relationships and a responsibility to consider how to take action to address injustices (Levinson, 2012). Rather than viewing individuals as isolated with "a predefined set of knowledge, skills and dispositions" (Biesta, 2007, p. 740), we emphasize democratic action in relation to others and to society and within the context of a supportive classroom, school, and community. A critical investigation also includes a consideration of who is participating, whose actions are considered worthy, whose voices are heard, and how such a lens may also bring to light ways in which social injustices might be ameliorated or perpetuated. Westheimer and Kahne (2004) outline the differences between civic education orientations that emphasize "making a difference" (p. 61) individually through civic acts and ethical choices, and programs that attend to broader interrogations of structural inequalities, warning that individualistic civic education programs may encourage participatory citizenship but may not encourage analysis of the root causes of social problems. Such an emphasis is not easy, however, and requires a balance between encouraging activities that can foster positive experiences of change and bolster agency and not sidestepping the investigation of controversial or complex causes and factors that perpetuate injustices and inequalities (Kahne & Westheimer, 2006).

STUDENT VOICE AND CIVIC AGENCY

The role of the student lies at the heart of civic engagement. This book pays attention to the ways in which young people are included in decisionmaking across school settings—often called student voice (Fielding, 2001; Mitra, 2005) in the literature—while also critically considering how participation may be more possible or recognized for some and not for others. The teachers and students in this book demonstrate ways in which their experiences helped them develop new identities as change makers and sources of support in the school. Such concepts are rarely explored in civic engagement research, and when they are examined, it is not done until the secondary school level (Flanagan & Faison, 2001; Lerner et al., 2005; Perkins & Borden, 2003).

Meaningful civic action within schools is rare, but has been shown to improve the lives of young people; students often become re-engaged in the school community and are also simultaneously more attached to their schools (Mitra, 2004). Through such deeper activities, when schools recognize student voice, young people report a stronger belief that they are capable of making a difference in their own lives and the lives of others (Eccles & Gootman, 2002; Mitra, 2004). At its best, civic action can lead to whole-school democratic structures and opportunities that model participatory practice (Apple & Beane, 2007; Serriere, Mayes, & Mitra, 2014). These actions can include service-learning (Serriere, McGarry, Fuentes, & Mitra, 2012; Wade, 2008), democratic deliberation to foster understanding of multiple perspectives (Mitra, 2008; Paley, 2009), classroom meetings in an atmosphere of perceived fairness and collective problem solving (Angell, 2004), youth participatory action research (Cammarota & Fine, 2008; Rubin & Jones, 2007), critical reflection of civic identities (Abu El-Haj, 2009), and youth organizing (Watts & Flanagan, 2007).

A CRITICAL SOCIOCULTURAL APPROACH TO MAKING A DIFFERENCE

Instead of a cognitive or developmental frame, this book embraces a critical sociocultural stance (Lewison, Leland, & Harste, 2008). It examines the conditions that enable young people to participate in democratic practices, including noticing and questioning injustices, developing critical questions, and examining ways in which structures and norms might leave out some voices and privilege others. Throughout this book, we show how the sociocultural conditions in which civic engagement occurs impact the quality and locus of engagement. We explore how children are active agents in the construction of their lives and social worlds (Mayall, 1994a). Rather than focusing on "becoming" citizens, we focus on and value the contributions that young people can make in the present day (Serriere, Mayes, & Mitra, 2014). Civic education, from this perspective, is not only about developing skills, knowledge, and attitudes for future participation, but also recognizes and values children as citizens in their own right, with standpoint knowledge about their current social and political communities (Osler & Starkey, 2005). Although these concepts focus on individual student development, for each idea, we stress how these assets are fostered through collective activities and further serve to strengthen the ability of young people to work together.

Previous research demonstrates that when students are given the opportunity for co-construction, they speak of developing shared meaning-making, learning to get along with others, exchanging perspectives, and working across differences (Mitra & Serriere, 2012; Sanders, Movit, Mitra, & Perkins, 2007). Practices presented in this book align with these findings. For example, we will show how philosophical dialogues with kindergartners at this school (discussed in Chapter 2) demonstrate children's capacity to engage empathically with others, offer reasons in support of their positions in discussion, and imagine beyond their own initial perspectives. The activities were not predetermined. In a spirit of inquiry, the answers offered were provisional and negotiable.

To understand the process of co-construction, we examine the sociocultural contexts that enable and constrain civic engagement, including ways in which some teachers and students might have greater opportunities for and interest in civic engagement activities and others may not. Voice alone does not always lead to engagement. Therefore, we highlight the diversity of teacher and student experiences at Dewey. We acknowledge that "student voice" is not a monolithic concept, but instead a vessel for a range of students' experiences and interactions. When we examine teacher empowerment, we note that not all teachers shared the same values, beliefs, or goals for civic engagement activities. It is the intersection of beliefs, lived experiences, and contexts in a social space that fosters conditions in which citizens seek to improve their own and others' conditions, or make a difference. As former elementary school teachers ourselves, we seek to connect with the experiences and perspectives of teachers, administration, parents, and students of education to frame this book in what we know is possible in schools through evidence and data, rather than a romantic vision of what schools could be.

A STRATEGIC CASE OF CIVIC ENGAGEMENT

The site of our research, Dewey Elementary, offers a strong example of a "typical" public school—one with curricular and socioeconomic challenges and one that wants to have a vision of education bigger than testing but feels pressure to narrow its curriculum and teach to the test. We also will describe how Dewey Elementary is unusual in how it responds to typical public school challenges. For 5 years, our research team engaged in extensive longitudinal case study (Yin, 1994) at Dewey Elementary School in the mid-Atlantic region of the United States, including conducting more than 450 observations and more than 50 interviews with groups and individual students, parents, teachers, and administration. Appendix A details our data collection and analysis strategies.

With 27% of students receiving free or reduced-price lunch, Dewey is not seen as advantaged locally; rather, it is a school that educates students from a range of socioeconomic backgrounds. The school struggled with making Adequate Yearly Progress (AYP) according to the state accountability guidelines and failed to do so one year during our data collection. Even in this context of threat, we describe how Dewey Elementary used that failure as an opportunity for inquiry and re-creating a discourse that supported its vision for education. Rather than succumbing to test pressure, the principal asked parents what should matter in their children's school, making a space to reframe the high-stakes testing discourse that framed Dewey as a "failing" elementary school.

The experiences of teachers, students, and administrators at Dewey offer key insights into how to construct a school focused on "making a difference" in one's school and the broader community (Mitra & Serriere, 2012). At Dewey, critical inquiry–based learning occurs when teachers respond to student voice, most often by encouraging students to explore their environment (and its injustices) through questions. These examples show how one must have agency to be able to make a difference. The inquiry process can facilitate changemaking by fostering connections between questioning injustice and civic responsibility and taking action. At Dewey, such activities often focused on environmental stewardship. For example, students asked: "Why don't we recycle milk bottles in our classrooms?" This question led to data collection on the number of bottles in each room and eventually a schoolwide classroom recycling effort. The student question "Why don't teachers compost their food like we do in the cafeteria?" led to students implementing composting in the teacher break room. In this way, students learned how to identify issues, collect data, and take action. Such inquiry processes created rich learning opportunities and reinforced the idea that the beliefs and opinions of young children mattered. When adults and students collaborate and listen to the voices of young people, they are more likely to set forth with agency, able to influence the actions of others.

Rather than initiating or being catalysts of civic engagement at Dewey Elementary, we positioned ourselves as guides on the side. We, the authors of this book, met as colleagues at Penn State University and soon after were invited to Dewey Elementary for an informal conversation by Principal Shannon. We realized that the three of us had many shared interests and beliefs in education and from there our shared professional work and relationship grew. After that initial meeting, we often attended Dewey functions, where we made casual inquiries about any civic initiatives in the school unfolding or occurring. This approach initially led us to studying the newly conceived Small School Advisories (SSA) initiative, and it later opened doors to many teachers' classrooms and other school activities. Although we do not align our approach with action research, we realize how our support of such work may have validated civic initiatives and encouraged them to continue. For instance, we noticed within the course of an action project led by 6 5th-grade girls, the ways our presence in meetings—although we were there just to take notes—seemed to encourage adults to take the girls' concerns with potentially more seriousness.

It is also important to point out that both of us as authors have personal and professional relationships with many of the teachers at Dewey and with Principal Shannon. Both of us regularly invite teachers and principal Shannon to be guest presenters in our university courses. Moreover, Stephanie has been co-teaching an elementary social studies methods course with Mrs. Howard for the last 5 years. At times, these relationships are also personal as our interest in community issues or events overlap.

Our pasts as teachers also shape our commitment to teachers, parents, principals, young students, and public schools. Before becoming researchers of schools, both authors were elementary school teachers. Stephanie's research and teaching focuses on elementary social studies methods, and often uses Dewey Elementary to frame examples in her course as a way to work within the pressures of accountability while still fostering meaningful, engaging, and experiential curriculum. Dana's research focuses on student voice, civic engagement, and school reform/ organizational change.

Moreover, as White women who have engaged in teaching and researching in diverse areas, we recognize and seek to uncover instances of privilege, including our own, and address inequities in schools. Part of this work, we believe, is supporting the public and civic mission of schools rather than looking toward privatized or charter schooling as a first option. As our subjectivity and positioning are also framed by our critical sociocultural lens, we mean to call attention to the ways in which power interacts in interrelated social, cultural, and geographic systems. This book captures ways in which children, teachers, parents, and school administration notice and deal with inequity, and seek to engage in social justice. Thus, although the work of civic engagement could be quite conservative (i.e. working to preserve the status quo), we seek to point out the ways in which endeavors at schools can be critical and transformative for society. While we remained open to issues of race and gender in our data collection and analysis, they were not always the most salient themes that emerged to explain the workings of power within voice, inquiry, and engagement.

It is also important to note that the examples we show in this book are not only filtered and analyzed in our conceptual and theoretical lenses, they are partial and not necessarily representative of the entire school. There are myriad examples at Dewey Elementary that we have left out, including examples of teachers in the school who may do less civic engagement work, or do not support this work at all. While we sought strategic examples of civic engagement that were potentially generative for thought and practice, at times we captured examples in this book that did not align with the research on best practices in civic education (i.e., the character education practice of introducing a "value of the week"). In as much, we aim to depict a realistic and complex portrayal of practices in this school culture.

All in all, the book shows how many teachers and leaders at Dewey school kept their vision despite external accountability pressures by finding ways to model civic learning and engagement while still responding to the increasing focus on mathematics and reading, "the twin engines driving the elementary school curriculum" (VanFossen, 2005, p. 377) in the United States. This book examines the mutually informing sociocultural spaces in which civic engagement can occur: the classroom, the school, and the community, as seen in Figure 1.1. We begin each section—(1) the classroom, (2) the school, and (3) the community—by giving an overview of what research in the field has demonstrated about civic engagement in that particular unit of space. We focus not just on learning civic skills, but on learning how to take civic action. Then, in each of the nested contexts, we describe cases in practice from within Dewey Elementary to portray in-depth examples and analysis of civic engagement, including how action can lead to academic, social, and civic learning. By using this model, we seek to navigate and explore multiple interacting systems. We did not intend to align the school or our framework with the often used "expanding horizons" approach in social studies education (see Halvorsen, 2009) that teaches children what is nearest to them first. Nor did we seek to draw parallels to Bronfenbrenner's (1994) ecological model of explaining children's development that is similar in the appearance of expanding concentric circles. Our focus calls attention to the mutually informing and contextual spaces within and around a school.

In Part I, we explore the classroom level. At Dewey, civic engagement begins as early as kindergarten, inviting children to consider others' perspectives and laying the foundation for teaching young people to identify issues of equity through philosophical thought (Chapter 2) and ameliorate injustice through service-learning (Chapter 3) and civic action projects (Chapter 4). In 2009, Dewey was honored with a prestigious national award for its exemplary practice of service-learning. Service-learning projects at Dewey Elementary pervade classrooms, including many with a focus on environmental stewardship. Three Dewey teachers designed curricula with the goal of fostering student-led civic engagement by morphing a prior scientific zine project (magazine-like folios made by students) into a civic action project around topics chosen by individual students (as described in Chapter 4). They have shared the pedagogy with other teachers, and the project has grown. Although academic knowledge is a primary goal in many of these projects, civic, scientific, and social learning are equally valued, though not areas not tested in the annual state test, as the data in Part I show.

Part II examines schoolwide initiatives, looking at the role of leadership, structures, and vision for creating spaces in which civic inquiries can grow. It begins with how scientific inquiry occurs in the "Schoolyard" initiative—a grant from the Department of Environmental Protection to continue fostering scientific inquiry about the school's gardens, wetlands, a composting area, and

Figure 1.1. Mutually Informing Spaces of Civic Engagement at Dewey Elementary

Community

School

Classroom

the woods (Chapter 5). Then, we describe another schoolwide civic initiative called All-School Assemblies (ASAs), which are schoolwide assemblies run by 5th-grade students (Chapter 6). These events serve as a platform for students to present projects to the whole student body, create a sense of school community, and provide the 5th-graders with leadership opportunities. In the next chapter, we present a third initiative, Small School Advisories (SSAs), or multiage advisories, which were introduced to ensure that all children developed a caring, stable relationship with an adult in school and to build community among students across grades (Chapter 7).

Part III examines how Dewey creates a community discourse that interacts and questions broader educational policies in ways that are unusual for an elementary school. We explore ways in which Dewey teachers, students, and administrators critically questioned their environment and sought to make changes. We also look at ways in which the Dewey community built bridges by partnering with other organizations and networks to both strengthen its own work and influence others. In chapters from this part, we examine how 5th-grade girls challenged the district lunch policy (Chapter 8), how teachers partnered with a local university to infuse inquiry-based practice into teacher education (Chapter 9), and ways in which teachers, administrators, and parents sought to call into question the state accountability assessments (Chapter 10).

We end each Part with considerations for practice in order to extend lessons from this particular school into other school contexts. A major goal of this book is not merely to present a unique school but to recognize the common struggles and triumphs of reclaiming democratic education across schools. Dewey Elementary therefore serves as a microcosm within today's public schools: a larger political landscape that challenges, but cannot overtake, the civic mission of public schools.

Part I

CLASSROOMS AS A SITE FOR CIVIC ENGAGEMENT

Civic engagement is fundamentally about fostering the conditions for people to live, work, and make decisions together in a diverse democracy. Elementary classrooms can serve as ideal spaces to create the conditions for engaged participation in such a democracy. We purposefully begin this book by exploring the practices within classrooms that work toward civic engagement.

Civic engagement is initiated within elementary classrooms in myriad ways. In U.S. contexts, classroom deliberations have been shown to occur within the earliest years (Ochoa-Becker, Morton, Autry, Johnstad, & Merrill, 2001). Indeed, eliciting students' opinions and voices has been conceptualized as a way to foster participation in pluralistic classrooms (Parker & Hess, 2001). Service learning as a platform for learning academic content and community engagement is one of the most common ways in which classrooms initiate civic action (Wade, 2008). According to the National Youth Leadership Council, service learning is "a philosophy, pedagogy, and model for community development that is used as an instructional strategy to meet learning goals and/or content standards" (2011, n.p.). Indicators of quality service learning that are modeled in this section include student voice, personal relevance, and students' understanding of societal issues being addressed.

When a conception of democracy is a form of "associated living" (Dewey, 1916), classrooms serve as an ideal place for learning through experience. Conversations in elementary classrooms often occur in the common area of the classroom rug, coined "circle time" in the United States and many other countries. Teachers use this space as a form of democratic deliberation and negotiation that we characterize as "carpet-time democracy" (Serriere, 2010). The use of classroom meetings has been found to promote deliberation, foster understanding of multiple perspectives, and encourage collective problem-solving (Angell, 2004). Indeed, opportunities to talk in class meetings can help students build positive relationships and a sense of identity within the group (Battistich, Solomon, Kim, Watson, & Schaps, 1995). In the early elementary years, "playtime in particular must be negotiated with a greater number and variety of others; new norms are introduced, and others must be improvised by the children themselves" (Parker, 2008, p. 69). Through teaching or action research, adults play a part in orchestrating diverse opinions, considerations, and status dynamics that pervade classrooms.

Perhaps the most renowned U.S. research of classroom discourse practice that seeks to foster early democratic participation is that of Vivian Paley (2009), who led conversations with her kindergartners, wondering aloud and together what their classroom would be like if children could agree on the social contract of "you can't say you can't play" to foster community and collaboration in the classroom. From the most immediate and personal issues of letting another person play in the block area to environmental issues such as fracking and global warming (Chapter 4), to the surprise of local homelessness (Chapter 3), these three chapters also highlight how social concerns raised in the classroom can become a platform for civic engagement, especially as teachers or leaders guide students through imaginative engagement with others' perspectives.

Still, the current educational political climate largely works against the possibilities of young people being agents of change within classrooms and defies much of the rhetoric that marginalizes children's "authentic" participation in the civic sphere, especially in the United States (Hart, 1992). Reports show that the majority of U.S. schools fail to provide an education for engaged citizenship (Kirshner, 2004; Larson, 2000), particularly at the elementary level (Boyle-Baise et al., 2008). An increased focus on accountability has focused attention away from both the learning and doing of citizenship in schools (Fitchett & Heafner, 2010).

Closely related to accountability efforts is a focus on the "one right answer" in classrooms. Within character education movements, studying the "value of the week" is a common way to teach children how to be good citizens in schools. This weekly value is usually illustrated by recognizing individual students in the school who embody the characteristic or value. These lessons often start and end with a desired outcome or demonstrable skill or value that students are expected to master (Howard, Berkowitz, & Schaeffer, 2004). Though popular in schools, a once-a-week discussion of a value is insufficient alone to teach civic engagement. Dewey also includes the "value of the week" exercises, but folds into these a wide array of civic actions and visions of children as changemakers. As John Dewey (1909) has pointed out, moral education can have two meanings. One is an effort to *produce* moral people, as in character education. The other is a way of being and learning in schools that is morally defensible. We see how Dewey Elementary holds the latter view. Children are not viewed as issues to fix, as if the problem lies within them. Rather, most adults at the school perceive the locus of injustice within schools as likely from high-stakes testing efforts within schooling. For this reason, we frame civic engagement as process based and dialogic, rather than teacher centered or didactic.

In a spirit of inquiry but counter to high-stakes testing efforts, we show how students at Dewey are able to offer answers that are provisional and negotiable. Students are encouraged to consider others' perspectives currently and historically and to revise their own opinions or perspectives. Working within Dewey Elementary, we acknowledge that these are rich but quite situated possibilities of working in classrooms with children for civic engagement. They are not meant to be exactly replicable, and yet they provide provocative examples of how to foster civic engagement. We realize that there are many other examples we did not choose to capture within Dewey Elementary and therefore bely complete representativeness of even this particular site.

We investigate children's participation to consider how to engage them in inquiry. As with any organic process, we highlight the unpredictability of their responses, and therefore the messiness of a democratic and civic-focused curriculum. We find that an emergent process-based approach with civics at the center fosters personal relevance and meaning for children. These examples demonstrate young children's capacities to think through challenging issues while remaining open to others' perspectives.

Findings on classroom meetings suggest that U.S. elementary students are capable of keeping an agenda and leading meetings in an atmosphere of perceived fairness and collective problem solving (Angell, 2004). Opportunities to talk in class meetings help students build positive relationships and a sense of identity within the group (Battistich & Horn, 1997). Open dialogues on classroom policies in early elementary years, from "carpet-time" talk to more formal classroom meetings run by students, help students consider conflicting priorities of self and others as well as practice a process of listening, deliberating, and considering all sides (Beck, 2005; Paley, 2009).

The recently published College, Career, and Civic Life (C3) Framework gives equal weight to the preparing students for an engaged civic life alongside college and career work. The curriculum framed by civic engagement at Dewey, described especially in Chapters 4 and 5, illustrates the possibilities within the C3 Framework's four domains: (1) developing questions and planning inquiries; (2) applying disciplinary concepts and tools; (3) gathering and evaluating sources to develop claims and use evidence; and (4) communicating conclusions and taking informed action. Moreover, this emphasis on skill building (rather than content alone) expands the role of *doing* rather than just *knowing*. By putting civic engagement (vis-à-vis service learning or civic zines) at the center of a classroom curriculum, this section demonstrates how schools and teachers can provide the youngest citizens with opportunities to connect with their local community and experience agency as citizens, starting in classrooms. Other scholars have argued that social studies is the most inclusive of all school subjects (Ross, 1997) as it studies "all human enterprise over time and space" (Stanley & Nelson, 1994, p. 266). Moreover, social studies includes civics as one of six social sciences. Placing meaningful and experiential civics as the center of planning, teaching, and learning in a classroom is a fuller translation of 'living one's civics' (Dunn, 1916) and integrating the social studies with language arts and other subjects. This section offers examples of the changing curricular landscape under the Common Core State Standards Initiative. By tending to a sociocultural climate of collectivity and process, we emphasize a public and democratic purpose in education, as well as the time and approach needed to re-create priorities within schools.

In this section, we begin with a chapter examining ways in which kindergartners engaged in philosophical dialogues (Chapter 2). The next chapter describes a 1st-/2nd-grade classroom whose interest in the local homeless shelter led to an extended and mutually beneficial partnership for learning and engagement (Chapter 3). In the final chapter of this section (Chapter 4), we describe a 5th-grade class and its engagements with a civic project in which students were invited to "make a difference." Throughout this book, we show how the sociocultural conditions in which civic engagement occurs impact the quality and locus of engagement. Similarly, we highlight how the conditions that foster civic engagement with children are as important as the action itself or the product of the action.

CHAPTER 2

Classroom Dialogue as a Platform for Civic Engagement

with Michael D. Burroughs

A focus on classroom dialogue serves as a collective and process-oriented means of expanding philosophical practice, encouraging perspective taking, and catalyzing civic action. In this chapter, open-ended and philosophical conversations around children's books highlight how even the youngest students can be deeply engaged in dialogue.

CIVIC ENGAGEMENT, DIALOGUE, AND PHILOSOPHY

Learning how to engage in dialogue is a key component of engagement in civic life through expression and consideration of a range of viewpoints (Parker, 2005). At its best, dialogue can be a shared inquiry on a matter of importance, including learning how to engage with a difference of opinions as well as differences in backgrounds, working styles, and cultures. Inherently, part of the work of civic engagement is developing shared meaning-making. Opportunities for dialogue can create mutual respect and opportunities for building common ground as well as a chance to understand conditions and life situations more clearly.

We use the term *dialogue* to describe a key mode of engaging young people in an experience of considering how we want to live together, rather than a sequenced lesson plan with predetermined outcomes for children or a need to reach consensus or agreement. We posit that perspective taking relates to empathy and is a critical process (rather than an isolated skill) in dialogue for civic engagement. Dialogue is a vital endeavor in enacting "we the people" in democracies. This practice is important because citizens "are not simply to exercise power (e.g., voting; direct action) but to think with one another about the power they exercise" (Parker & Hess, 2001, p. 282). Thus, citizens should engage with one another in dialogue to realize that their actions do not only impact themselves (and involve our rights), but also impact others (and involve responsibility). Parker (2005) points out that the original meaning of the word *idiocy* equated to *private, separate, self-centered,* or *selfish,* and was a term of reproach in ancient Greek culture. Dialogue, on the other hand, is communal and depends on considering what is right or wrong and others' realities. As we engage in dialogue in classrooms, we often consider "What should we do?" or ways we want to be together (Developmental Studies Center, 1996). As in the seminal example portrayed by Vivian Paley (2009), who led her kindergartners in a yearlong debate on instituting the rule "You can't say you can't play," students bring various personal and public reasons to the conversation to discuss what is fair or unfair in their shared lives. Dialogue is a key practice and experience for civic engagement in a democracy, but most of the research and practice on youth's capacity to engage in dialogue occurs at the older years (Hess, 2009; Mitra, 2004). We frame dialogue alongside philosophical practices in civic engagement to highlight a process orientation, unlike deliberation that usually results in deciding the "best" course of action (Parker, 2005).

In this and other Dewey Elementary classrooms, dialogue serves as a springboard to engage children in philosophical thought and civic engagement with one another. Historically, dialogue has played a central role in philosophical practice. In the work of historical philosophers ranging from Plato to Immanuel Kant, dialogue is used as a central means for investigating philosophical questions and gaining knowledge. In addition, many contemporary philosophers have focused on the educative qualities of dialogue and the importance of its inclusion in K–12 education (Haynes, 2008; Lipman, 2003; Matthews, 1992; Mohr Lone, 2012). In dialogue, the sharing of thoughts or feelings (the end point of many traditional classroom conversations) acts as a starting point, a beginning to an ongoing discernment and exploration of concepts, ideas, and questions through inquiry. Students and teachers sustain this process as they seek out truth and meaning relating to the subject under consideration. As Joanna Haynes (2008) notes:

> [Dialogue] is so much more than just sharing ideas and airing opinions. There is a dynamic orientation and draw implicit in dialogue. It is concerned with collaboratively solving problems, resolving dilemmas, developing new ways of thinking and understanding: rigorous searches for "truth." (p. 143)

The aims of dialogue at Dewey Elementary are inextricably tied to a style of pedagogy in which students and teachers engage in open discussion on a chosen prompt (text, question, idea, and so on), raise claims, arguments, and counterarguments, and seek to construct knowledge as a group. Dialogue flourishes when students and teacher engage in a "cooperative enquiry" such that they can challenge one another, question, appeal to reasons, and revise positions as needed (Fisher, 2007). Although useful for some educational purposes, other pedagogical strategies—conversation, monologue, and recitation, for example—lack these aims, as well as the reciprocal sharing of ideas and questions that is essential to dialogical communication. Dialogue (and related forms of questioning and critical reflection) at Dewey Elementary often positions children as active participants in the classroom and their own education more generally.

Dialogue has also been used in the service of various foci and fields in elementary schools such as Gay, Lesbian, Bisexual and Transsexual (GLBT) discussions (Bickmore, 1999), scientific practice (Jacobs, Herrenkohl, & McCrohon, 1998), and teacher–child and child–child interactions through journals for the service of reading and writing (Gambrell, 1985). The process and pedagogy of these fields share elements across subject areas that benefit from dialogue. A focus on classroom dialogue serves as a collective and process-oriented means of expanding philosophical practice, encouraging perspective taking, and catalyzing civic action.

Typically, young children do not engage in sustained democratic and philosophical dialogue on their own, but rather with teacher scaffolding and within sociocultural conditions that allow for responsiveness. Engaging in productive collective discussions around powerful texts has long been a goal of teachers (Parker & Hess, 2001). Specifically, children's literature is a longstanding entry point to and mode of scaffolding adult–child dialogue about social life. The images and scenarios in children's books represent larger social and philosophical issues and engage the ethical sensitivities of children as they relate the stories and characters to their world. Photographic images of critical incidents in their classroom may also be a means/platform for dialogue on social issues with young children (Serriere, 2010). Like many text-based looking and talking activities, reading and looking at storybooks at Dewey serves as a familiar yet flexible cultural format for children. Although the story reading format sets up some expectations about call and response, contributing to answers and posing new issues, we also observed how it fosters rich student-to-student as well as teacher-to-student interactions.

FOSTERING IMAGINATIVE ENGAGEMENT IN OTHERS' WORLDS

The focal point of Mrs. S.'s kindergarten classroom is a large carpeted area punctuated by a rocking chair, a calendar, and a whiteboard. At the edges of the carpet, four tables serve as a space for students' group-work, rather than individual desks. A bean-shaped table sits near one wall as a workspace for a teacher's assistant who meets with small groups of children. Mrs. S.'s desk is at the far window side of room. The space is characteristic of most kindergarten classrooms housed within an elementary school, and similar to many in which we have taught and observed where reading and writing is the main focus, with some time for units that incorporate social studies, science, and math.

The children sit down in front of Dr. Burroughs, a visiting public philosopher and professor, with drawings in hand. While we later describe Dr. Burroughs and his relationship to the school in more depth, we focus here on a vignette with children engaged in philosophical discussions with him. Burroughs sits in the teacher's rocking chair at the front of the carpeted area. Burroughs asks the children to share their drawings with a partner. Mrs. S. helps some straggling students find a partner.

To continue the conversations, Burroughs introduces the book *Hey, Little Ant* (Hoose, Hoose, & Tilley, 1998) to the kindergartners. The book depicts a tiny ant that is in danger of being stepped on by a young boy. The book suspends the deciding moment of whether or not the boy will step on the ant. The ant begs the boy not to kill him and gives reasons why he should be spared. In turn, the boy ponders the ant's guilt (the ant previously stole food from picnics) and the worth of the ant's life.

Burroughs leads the kindergartners in questioning and considering the right thing for the boy to do (should he step on the ant or not?). Throughout the discussion, the kindergartners raise questions and ideas about additional aspects of the story and the ethical dilemma it presents.

Several pages into the book, Burroughs pauses and asks the kids to close their eyes and imagine how the ant might be feeling while in danger. Later, he asks them to consider how the boy is feeling:

Burroughs: How do you think the boy is feeling?
Kate: Happy.
Carrie: Mad. He doesn't like ants and he wants to squish it.
Jade: Angry.
Rose: They [the ant and the boy] both have feelings.
Burroughs: Like Rose said, the boy and the ant are alike. Do we all agree with Rose?

In this instance, some children raise their hand to agree with Rose. Others keep their hands down. One student expands on why he agrees with Rose that ants and humans are "alike." Other students, one after another, add reasons why they agree with Rose:

Patrick: They both have a life.
Jack: They have eyes, hands, feet, and [a] back.
Ebony: Maybe they both feel scared.
Michelle: They are both animals [to repeat Rose].

Following a discussion of similarities between the ant and boy (including their respective feelings), Burroughs returns to reading the book. Prompted by the book and student questions, the class begins to consider whether or not the ant is a "crook," which, in part, is why the boy is considering stepping on him. Focusing on the ant, Burroughs asks, "Is it okay to kill a crook?" After some silence, Burroughs then asks, "Who thinks the ant is doing something wrong?" Six children raise their hand.

Tim: (raising his hand) It's not nice to steal.
Jack: You can't take some food. That's stealing.
Eric: I think it's in the middle because they only have no food left. The ant is in the middle. There's stealing but probably they don't have a lot of food.

In this last line, Eric offers a new direction in the discussion and an evaluation of stealing that is complex and between right and wrong. We found this moment significant in the dialogue because it complicated the binary of right/wrong and helped the students discover how ethical dilemmas can be complicated—more than one choice may be correct and none of the choices may feel quite right. In addition, it revealed the child's ethical awareness and his ability to discern the potential complexity of ethical decisions and competing values (for example, caring versus justice).

Rather than focusing on a desired outcome or demonstrable skill or value that students were expected to master, the dialogue prompted issues and tensions in the book that are common to life in a diverse society. The children not only discussed those tensions (right or wrong), but also went further by grappling with larger societal issues such as killing and retributive justice.

This example also highlights the importance of students' perspective taking in the dialogue, both with one another and with characters in the book. Initially, Burroughs asked the students to close their eyes and use their imagination to put themselves in the ant's place. They later did the same for the opposing character in the book, the boy. This process, as elements of it are repeated regularly in his discussions, allows for imaginative engagement with others' worlds. Perspective taking seemed to foster initial empathy for the ant's position and then, in turn, for the boy's. Children agreed and disagreed with one another about the feelings of the ant and the boy, and several settled on being "in the middle" regarding the ant's act of stealing (that is, whether this act was right or wrong). This example may do some work to dispel the notion that kids are incapable of doing meaningful dialogical work, or, further, that they are unable to imagine beyond their own perspectives. Instead, from a young age children can reason in complex ways, are capable of considering others' perspectives, and recognize the potential for ambiguity in moral judgment and evaluation. These abilities are evident in the dialogue examples above, as well as in additional contributions made by the kindergartners throughout the session relating to ethics ("If it is not yours, do not take anything" and "It is not nice to steal something out from other people") and empathy ("You can see he [the ant] just wants food" and "I would tell him [the boy] not to squash me out of life").

In addition, this discussion demonstrates the value of introducing collaborative civic, philosophical, and ethical discussions with young children. As opposed to predetermining the outcome of the discussion (for example, by structuring all questions and deciding on all discussion points in advance), teachers can aim to create an "open space" for children to act as collaborators in classroom dialogue. The creation of this space begins with the use of child-centered discussion prompts (such as children's literature, artwork, and authentic questioning) and continues with a teacher leader scaffolding student questions, comments, and contributions. When successful, the children emerge as key actors in and co-constructors of classroom dialogue. Through their salient points and questions—in the example above, regarding the act of stealing and the respective feelings of the boy and ant—the structure and focus of the dialogue begins to take shape. In this fluid process, student questioning, listening, and respectful discussion are just as important as "right answers." The result, then, is an active and engaged group of students and, in general, the creation of a robust community of inquiry in the kindergarten classroom.

CIVIC ENGAGEMENT AS DIALOGUE

Civic engagement is fundamentally about fostering the conditions for people to work, live, and make decisions together in a democracy. At Dewey, one of the first building blocks to foster civic engagement is encouraging dialogue in kindergarten classrooms. Principal Shannon invited a partnership with two local university representatives affiliated with the Department of Philosophy. From initial conversations, Principal Shannon found that she shared a belief with the two—a senior lecturer and a graduate student. Philosophical, civic, and ethical discussions should have a prominent place in early childhood education. Prior to these guest teachers leading book dialogues at Dewey, students and teachers were already engaging in weekly conversations on citizenship values such as "responsibility," "cooperation," and "community." The partnership with philosophers extended this established practice at Dewey by adding facilitated discussions of philosophical and ethical concepts, additional forms of discussion prompts (for example, children's literature and artwork), and structured scaffolding of student dialogue.

We purposefully began this book with an example of kindergartners in philosophical discussion to exemplify young people's engagement in classroom civic life and to push back against the notion of civic engagement as merely character education at a young age. The "value of the week" is one common way to teach children how to be good citizens in schools. A student or group of students being recognized for demonstrating the characteristic or value usually accompanies this strategy. Lessons often start and end with a desired outcome or demonstrable skill or value that students are expected to master. As will be shown in Chapter 8, whereas the majority of Dewey teachers do not utilize the value of the week strategy alone, a small percentage of Dewey teachers embrace an approach to teaching for an outcome of students embracing weekly "citizenship" values.

Here we show that instead of a predetermined approach, dialogues with children can be emergent, not predetermined. In a spirit of inquiry, answers offered are provisional and negotiable. Through an extended example from a kindergarten classroom at Dewey, we frame the rich but situated possibilities of dialogue with children. We investigate children's capacity to engage empathically with others, offer reasons in support of their positions in discussion, and imagine beyond their own initial perspectives. We find that an emergent, process-based approach fosters student voice and the seeds of social and civic inquiry for children. This approach also demonstrates the usefulness of thinking through challenging issues while remaining open to others' opinions.

Practicing the skills needed to learn how to "make a difference" can begin in the earliest grades. Rather than viewing children as "adults in the making," the experiences in this kindergarten classroom demonstrate ways in which young people are already capable of being active agents in the construction of their lives and social worlds (Mayall, 1994a), with valued knowledge about these worlds (Mayall, 2000). Civic education, from this perspective, is not only about developing the skills, knowledge, and attitudes for future participation, but also recognizes and values children as citizens in their own right, with standpoint knowledge about their current social and political communities (Osler & Starkey, 2005). This perspective also calls for further exploration of and active listening to how young people think about their civic education and their capacity to "make a difference" in the world (Graham & Fitzgerald, 2010), describing and participating in citizenship and efficacy on their own terms (Flacks, 2007).

Kindergartners at Dewey engage in ethical discussions about justice and care, demonstrating that they are capable of empathy and able to consider themselves change agents in their own worlds. By leading with an example of kindergartners doing philosophy, we reject the notion that young people are incapable of considering others' perspectives at an early age or are naturally "egocentric," as some early developmental theorists have assumed (Kohlberg, 1984; Piaget, 1997). We offer counterevidence to these historical presumptions and discourses on children to demonstrate that even at a young age there is rich potential in engaging children in the work of living together in a democracy. In fact, considering others' perspectives and values at a young age has been described as a "springboard" for empathy development in early childhood (Hoffman, 2001). And, further, numerous contemporary developmental researchers acknowledge that children possess ethical concerns and the capacity for moral judgment from a young age (Killen & Smetana, 2014; Nucci, 2001; Smetana, 1981).

By connecting ideas with approachable children's literature, students deliberated ethical issues, practiced coming to consensus, and learned to disagree. During a day's work on the book *Frog and Toad Are Friends* (Lobel, 1970), the class considered whether it is ever okay to tell your friend a lie (for instance, telling your friend you are not home when you actually are home). The children voiced various opinions about this, considered others, and changed their minds. "Toad is lying to Frog," said one child. "No, he is just tricking him," said another. Another child explained, "Well, he really just didn't want to play that day." The students failed to come to a consensus but then turned to a general ethical issue—are there times when lying is not wrong? Although the children clearly looked forward to the book itself, questions like these sparked excited conversations about friendship, honesty, and justice.

Rather than finding philosophical discussions intimidating, the kindergartners seemed thirsty for these conversations, often bubbling with energy and focus on the topic at hand. The discussions occurred on the large carpeted area of the two kindergarten classrooms. With the children sitting on the rug anywhere they liked, the teacher leaders usually sat on a rocking chair so all the children could see them and the children's book they were reading. If any physical or intellectual shifts occurred during these activities, it was a celebration of intellectual playfulness, stepping away from serious-minded work. The children conversed at length with one another and the teacher leaders about dilemmas presented in the selected books chosen because they contain ethical and philosophical dilemmas.

LESSONS FOR PRACTICE

We cannot expect children to practice being democratic and ethical citizens if their entire educational experience models autocracy. On the other end, not all teachers may feel comfortable exploring ethical issues with ease alongside children. It is our hope that this chapter illustrates ways in which teachers and children might promote the idea of dialogue with one another on immanent ethical, philosophical, and civic concepts and questions (for more on fostering dialogue through children's literature see Haynes & Murris, 2011; Mohr Lone, 2012; Wartenberg, 2013). This experience can be complemented with additional discussion and evaluation of classroom rules and aspects of the social life of the classroom. Based on our teaching and research in classrooms, we offer the following considerations for practice.

Shift the focal point of the class to co-collaboration when fostering dialogue with young students. Students can learn most effectively when their interests, ideas, and concerns are made central to classroom lessons. Children are motivated and, in turn, become more self-directed learners when they are included as co-collaborators in the learning process. In opposition to teacher-centered (or "banking") pedagogy (Freire, 2000), dialogical pedagogy requires that students contribute to discussion and the development of knowledge, thereby gaining confidence as active epistemic agents in the classroom. Teachers become co-learners and facilitators rather than transmitters of knowledge. Teachers encourage student contributions as much as possible, both through the use of child-centered discussion prompts (such as engaging activities, children's literature, and artwork) and consistent encouragement.

Model the questioning and critical reflection. Teachers might encourage questioning in their students by first appearing "as a questioner" themselves (Lipman, Sharp, & Oscanyan, 1980, p. 103). By acknowledging their own fallibility as knowers and asking students to assist them and one another in the dual process of learning and knowing, teachers provide a space for civic, philosophical, and ethical inquiry to take root. Teachers can accomplish this in numerous ways—from being open about their own uncertainty in regard to the questions under consideration to, when possible, introducing open-ended questions instead of declarative statements (for example, "What reasons do we have for believing X?"; "What do you mean by X?"; "Why do you agree/disagree with X?").

Discuss the importance of "care" and "respect" in the classroom explicitly during class meetings. Through this discussion, the teacher, along with students, can help create a classroom in which vulnerability and openness are sources of opportunity and shared learning. When we share ideas and questions with others, we are, at the same time, making a request; we are asking to be heard, to be taken seriously as a knower and collaborator. To be overly critical or flippant in the face of these offerings (questions, ideas, arguments, and so forth) can be taken as rejection and can have a detrimental impact on a student's self-confidence, sense of inclusion, and willingness to engage in dialogue.

Develop rules collaboratively to encourage and support productive dialogue. Establishing norms matters. It takes intention to model and teach inclusive conversation. Other norms include active listening, perspective taking, arguing with evidence, and sharing resources. During initial class meetings, the group can select guidelines or rules that will help structure productive discussions. These guidelines can develop from group consideration of forms of interaction that will best support discussion and communication (for example, listening, speaking, and being heard by others). By facilitating an opening discussion on "good discussions," the teacher opens a space for class members to consider and nominate conditions of a successful dialogue. Students can then think about what they take to be the most important rules to support dialogue, whether these might be "listening when a classmate speaks," "being respectful of all class members," or "asking a question when you don't understand a comment" (or something else entirely).

Provide "scaffolding" for the discussion through various facilitation techniques. For example, throughout the discussion the facilitator can ask clarification questions ("When you say X, do you mean . . . ?"), restate student comments for clarification ("Did we all hear Bryan? He said . . ."), and provide encouragement ("That's very insightful. Does anyone else have something to add?"). On a related note, this work must be valued through the time given to it and its place in the schedule.

Believe that kids are change agents now, not just agents for the future. Believing in kids involves leaning into what they can think about *and* what they can do (both action and thought). Fostering civic agency toward fulfilling engagement with young people occurs while scaffolding both their thoughts and their actions. Because our expectations of children frame much of what children accomplish in schools, we can work to expect them to think deeply and listen for it in dialogue.

Be present as a listener. Listening to those who are less heard in society serves as an ethical component of dialogue. It takes practice to be a good listener for children and to push away from accepting the position of being the one who determines right and wrong or moving efficiently along to the next item on our day's agenda.

Name an intellectually playful space for students. A teacher leader might wish to explicitly name and mark this conversation as a *different and more playful* space compared with times in the school day that are focused on learning facts and providing "correct" answers. Because high-stakes testing often positions children as passive recipients of knowledge, encouraging dialogue and the cultivation of diverse opinions, knowledge, and forms of evidence must be purposefully framed.

Embrace the challenge of meaningful dialogue. Discussion can be a difficult pedagogical feat. As we embark on the path to dialogical engagement with students, it is important to know that it might not be easy or seamless. Dialogue takes practice; it can be messy. Moreover, it will take time for future teachers to master this practice (Parker & Hess, 2001), and it will never be perfect. Social studies scholars Parker and Hess remind us that they do not "know anyone who claims to be an expert discussion leader, and those who are demonstrably very good at it speak mainly of their deficiencies" (p. 273). As expressed humbly and eloquently by Maxine Greene (1954, as quoted in Parker & Hess, 2001), discussion is an incredibly difficult pedagogical feat," says one of them, "which I, for one, have never in my life pulled off to my entire satisfaction. I have never conducted a discussion of which I could honestly credit myself with a grade of more than 75 out of 100. (p. 36)

Despite its messiness, the work of engaging in dialogue and civic education with young people is important and justifiable. According to Parker (2005):

> Educators are justified in shaping curriculum and instruction toward the development of democratic citizens. In poll after poll, the American public makes clear its expectation that schools do precisely this. As it turns out, schools are ideal sites for democratic citizenship education. The main reason is that a school is not a private place, like our homes, but a public, civic place with a congregation of diverse students. (p. 347)

In sum, engaged citizens do not materialize out of thin air. Public schools are the site for young citizens to learn to engage in productive, thoughtful, and democratic ways and "a proper curriculum for democracy" necessitates "both the study and the practice of democracy" (Parker, 2005, p. 350). Engaging in collective and emergent dialogue in children's early experiences in school is an important first and continual practice for life in a democracy, and especially within a democratic school.

"Children Live There!?"

Empathy, Perspective Taking, and Service Learning with the Local Homeless Shelter

Seeing the world beyond one's own view and imagining others' perspectives, opinions, and experiences is one of the most important skills in being an active and responsible citizen. According to American sociologist C. Wright Mills (2000), the *sociological imagination* is a capacity to shift from one perspective to another—it applies imaginative thought to the asking and answering of sociological questions such as those presented in this chapter: *Are there homeless people in our small Pennsylvania valley? What can we, even as 1st- and 2nd-graders, do to help?* Fostering a sociological imagination promotes perspective taking, a key democratic skill in solving real-world problems, collectively and reciprocally.

FRAMING SERVICE LEARNING

One of the most common entry points to civic engagement in schools is service learning, which combines civic and other academic disciplines through an experience within or for a community. It is endorsed by both conservatives and liberals, albeit for different rationales (see Kahne & Westheimer, 1996). Service learning can give purpose to academic learning because it allows young citizens to procure a sense of agency, purpose in their work, connection to their community, and an expanded perspective.

Dewey teachers embraced service learning as a common practice and part of the school's identity. Dewey Elementary was awarded national grant monies to support service learning in the school and was named a "School of Success" by State Farm for its existing commitment to service learning with its students interacting with the local and global communities. Although the teachers at Dewey report that they rarely need money to conduct service learning in their classrooms, the award buoyed classroom and schoolwide efforts in service learning. Because of the grant, several teachers and Principal Shannon became leaders of service learning within the school district, delivering professional development workshops for district teachers and administrators and within undergraduate university teacher education classes, as well as establishing a page on the district's website to display

service-learning practices. Principal Shannon emphasized the importance of max-
imizing the independence of teachers to shape their teaching to align with their
own talents and student needs. She noted:

> They could do service-learning as a part of Small School Advisories
> [discussed in Chapter 7], or with a piece of curriculum . . . anywhere
> students disengage from their curriculum. . . . It'll come out for some people
> there because that's their *modus operandi* to get kids hooked and engaged.
> Other people will do it in their classroom. Others will at least know what it
> is and not complain about others doing it—which would be my goal. If you
> don't want to participate, fine, but get out of our way.

Service learning at Dewey Elementary is a pedagogy usually initiated at the
classroom level by teachers. It impacts the school community, the town's community, and even beyond. Dewey Elementary's All-School Assemblies served as a
space to initiate support for and to celebrate service learning projects. This chapter illustrates the way service-learning offers opportunities for young students to
express their capabilities in perspective taking and imagining others' realities. In
her first year of teaching, Stacey Benson taught a mixed age class of 1st- and 2nd-
graders at Dewey. She engaged her students in local service learning by following
their burgeoning interest in homelessness.

DEFYING EGOCENTRISM

Traditionally, the elementary social studies curriculum has followed an "expanding horizons" approach in which students learn about that which is closest to
them (self, community) and then move outward (city, state, country) in space
(Halvorsen, 2009). This traditional framework for civics and social studies in the
elementary years grows from the work of developmental scholars who positioned
children as naturally egocentric and incapable of considering others' perspectives
of the world around them (see, for example, Davies, 2004; Piaget, 1951; Vygotsky,
1978). In this logic, young people are capable of understanding only something
they have experienced or is near to themselves. However, research in gender and
ethnic identity (Ruble, Martin, & Berenbaum, 1998) shows that young children
are capable of taking on the roles of others and understanding how their own decisions affect others. Considering others' realities at a young age has been described
as the basis, or "springboard," for having a lifetime of empathy (Hoffman, 2001)
and the foundation for being effective and participant in public spaces.

Stacey Benson's mode of teaching, described in this chapter, defies this developmental logic about young students' egocentric nature: Students became fas-
cinated by homelessness first as a global phenomenon and then moved closer to
"home" in their understanding of it, moving in the opposite trajectory of the "expanding horizons" approach. This example shows that classrooms are ideal spaces

to learn to live among one another, being able to see others' perspectives on the world and empathize with other people. Children, like adults, encounter difficult issues when it comes to learning to live together in a shared space. Rather than suggesting a developmental logic to explain any lack of empathy in children, we underscore the way teachers can create norms for perspective taking that can allow for expressions of empathy in ways not necessarily expected from children. This case of Benson's class shows how inquiry and empathy pave the way for civic engagement.

It was Stacey Benson's first year of teaching. She described her mixed age 1st-/2nd-grade class at the beginning of the year as particularly tough because "they were a class with some 'meanness' issues." She went on to say that many students in her class had been "struggling with self-centered behaviors like cutting in line, name-calling, and purposefully ostracizing students on the playground." Mrs. Benson, who aimed foremost for a classroom climate that fostered learning and cooperation, felt disappointed. She began to hold regular class meetings on the carpet with her 1st- and 2nd-graders to talk through how they could be inclusive and get along better on the playground. Students shared their perspectives, but for several months the problems that occurred regularly on the playground were evident in classroom life, too.

Academically, Mrs. Benson started the year with a unit on habitats, a typical unit in the district that led her students to atypical ends: an entire year of study about homes and homelessness. She explained that it was natural to connect the idea of animal habitats to human habitats: "It's not just food, water, shelter, but *healthy* food, *clean* water, and *protective* shelter *for all living things*." To make this animal–human habitat connection initially, she read a popular children's book, *Fly Away Home* (Bunting, 1991), about a man and his son who end up homeless and living at an airport. During a discussion about the book, one of her students shared that he had visited New York City and seen homeless people begging for money. Another student said that she had been to China and seen homeless people there as well. Mrs. Benson recalled that the children were "absolutely amazed" and engaged with these stories about human "habitats," especially with regard to this issue of homelessness. Yet, with examples from only a children's book, New York City, and China, the children perceived homeless people to be far away and scary.

PLANNING A SERVICE-LEARNING PROJECT

Benson wanted to help her students connect their questions about homelessness and healthy human "habitats" to their local community. After some thinking, she decided to contact a student's mother who served on the board of the local homeless shelter, Easton House. This practice of partnering with local organizations to create relationships for service-learning projects is a common practice at Dewey Elementary. Dewey teachers have found that some organizations need more help than others conceptualizing how elementary students might be of assistance to their organization. The classroom benefited from a mother of a student in the class serving as the liaison with the community organization. She understood the needs of the organization and the capabilities of the children in the class as well.

Despite her initial apprehension as a 1st-year teacher, Mrs. Benson followed her students' interest in the topic and invited the mother, Joanna, to speak to the class about Easton House. Benson knew that Joanna had approached Principal Shannon previously to let her know she was interested in connecting Easton House with a classroom at Dewey. When Joanna visited, the students learned that many people come to Easton House in times of need and that the shelter can hold up to 19 people, depending on the families' configuration. One student asked, as if to confirm, "So this is here, in Easton?" Benson later described that moment when they realized there was a homeless shelter in their town:

> When Joanna came in and talked to us and showed us pictures of Easton House. In *our town*!!?? Just this *horror* came over their faces. And it was like, in my room of 14 active and vocal boys, you could hear a pin drop, you know?

It was clear that most of the students had never suspected there were homeless people in their own comfortable, university town in the Midwestern United States. After all, the town was nicknamed "Pleasant Valley" because of its imperviousness to hardship during the Great Depression and, more recently, because it had fared relatively well in the country's economic downturn.

The students examined photos of the inside of Easton House and saw that it had once been a professor's home. In this class conversation, students commented that the building no longer felt "homey" or "cozy," particularly in contrast with their own homes decorated during the holiday season. The children knew intuitively as they examined the photos of the shelter that a "home" should have a particular look and feel, aesthetically. This conversation, augmented with photos of the house, got children thinking more directly about the lives of the people in the shelter.

To add a "homey" touch to Easton House, the children sat outdoors to draw a winter scene from their school's yard and to write about the outdoors using descriptive language. They took these renderings indoors to create watercolor paintings, and they used their writing to make "list poems" to accompany their art. These paintings and poems were then laminated and made into placemats for the residents to make things more "homey" at Easton House. Mrs. Benson described what followed:

> We did winter decorations and stuff like that. And then going forward, they're starting to ask more questions. "Well, don't they need other things? Don't they need other things around their house? Don't they need toilet paper and trash bags and toothbrushes and stuff like that? How can we get those things for them?"

Mrs. Benson reported being somewhat surprised at all these concerned questions, considering her students' more selfish behavior at the beginning of the school year. As the children imagined the lives of others and put themselves in those people's shoes, they were less concerned about getting "more" for themselves and more concerned with helping others. The tone of the class shifted. In the face of an identified community problem, these same students were showing a more caring side, something that would become even more evident as the academic year progressed.

Mrs. Benson encouraged the emerging service project, leading the class to brainstorm possible ways they could help Easton House. Drawing on Joanna's knowledge as a representative of Easton House, the class asked questions about the residents' needs. They brainstormed solutions that took those needs into account. After learning that Easton House had limited refrigerator space, they revised their idea about providing fresh fruits and vegetables into making healthful, nonperishable trail mixes. Students also learned that the residents did not have room to accept donations of clothing or games but that they did appreciate winter decorations to make their place more home-like. Benson explained how she sought to let the project come from students' ideas, allowing her to take a "scaffolded" approach of steering them toward successful ends.

As these ideas emerged, Mrs. Benson's students interviewed their own families about how and when they came to live in Easton. Students conducted oral histories by constructing interview questions and collected answers from parents, grandparents, and other family members in the area. In sharing their interview data with the class, several students saw clear themes emerging about circumstances that affect family life, such as job changes, community safety, and family health. They began to make connections between the changes in their own families and how their local community—including Easton House—had changed over the years.

This intellectual and imaginative capacity to recognize the values, circumstances, and decisionmaking of people in the past has been described as *historical empathy* (Barton, 2008; Davis, Yeager, & Foster, 2001), which we relate to the students' broader capacities of perspective taking. While they were thinking locally and historically about homes, the students completed a "free-write" on what they liked about their homes. Although they started by thinking about homes and homelessness as being far away and different from their own homes, they discovered that they shared something quite local with the residents of Easton House: a history and a town.

APPLYING DISCIPLINARY CONCEPTS AND TOOLS:
PUTTING CIVICS AT THE CENTER

As a 1st-year teacher, Stacey Benson was excited but overwhelmed—she wanted to find time for her students to work on the service project, but she also had to make sure she was covering the standards for the year. Surprisingly, she found myriad curricular connections, and, instead of artificially "tacking on" integrations here and there, civic engagement via service learning became the core of the curriculum, promoting deeper connections and conceptual understandings across subject areas. Once she began looking broadly at her curriculum through the lens of the budding service-learning project around Easton House, she found numerous connections in reading, writing, social studies, science, and math. She created a chart to organize the ways in which she would integrate the project into the curriculum while following the iterative steps of service learning. These steps include: identify a problem, investigate it, research solutions, implement project, celebration evaluation, and reflection. Using these steps as one axis of her chart, she described in the opposite columns the curricular connections she could make at each step. Instead of teaching service learning as an "add-on," she put the project at the center of the curriculum and worked outward. Two other teachers in her school reported that they were "impressed" at her fast learning curve in terms of incorporating service learning into her repertoire, while other more experienced teachers were still "starting small." Benson explained her perspective on how she developed the project:

> I think, you know, the other teachers saw it, too, and were like, "Well, how did you figure this out?" Well, it's like right there if you're looking for it, you know? Those connections in the books are all there, it's all there, if you have the project in mind. It wasn't rocket science at all, but I think we've been able to walk them through it so they've been able to discover it on their own so they realize it's a problem and figure out what to do about it.

Soon after the project ended, Benson was invited to present this class project to preservice teachers at the local university. When the preservice teachers expressed their concerns about service learning taking up too much time, she explained:

> But we weren't doing the service project all day, every day. It was something we came back to quite often, though. And when we didn't touch base with it for a few weeks over the winter, students began to ask when they were going to do something for Easton House again.

In this way, she focused on addressing academic standards through the engaging, authentic, and student-driven vehicle of service learning. As she brought each curricular discipline with its unique concepts, tools, and skills to life through the project, she soon discovered that intentionally integrating service into the curriculum with a larger purpose had more than academic outcomes. She didn't expect the social and civic results to be palpable so soon in her own classroom climate.

The value and importance of taking another person's perspective suddenly became apparent even in mathematics. While the students were making the trail mix for Easton House, Benson offered a way of understanding basic fractions (a math standard) through dividing ingredients and trail mix baggies for residents.

The students were excited about making sure the bag contents were "fair," or evenly divided for residents. Their understanding proved to her that they not only "got it [fractions]," but they were much more engaged than they had been when she'd explained fractions previously on the whiteboard. "They had a purpose for learning it," she added. Later, when they divided food into baskets for the Easton House residents, the children were especially motivated to make sure that the goods were evenly distributed because they knew that one resident would not want to get less than the others. Moreover, Benson shared, "Division used to be something 'hard' that 4th-graders did. Now my students were understanding what division meant and why it was so important." Division, in the context of this project, meant equality and fairness to them.

Their project began as a unit on "habitats," mostly on animals, but as students considered how all living things need healthful food, clean water, and protective shelter appropriate for them, the students made rich connections to the needs of humans, and more precisely how animal and human habitats relate. Mrs. Benson articulated her satisfaction with this route: "This has been really rewarding because I had an image in my head of where we can go, and it's taken us in different places." They considered the healthful needs of the Easton House residents by recognizing that they needed healthy, nonperishable snacks. Then, they applied their study of a science unit on solids and liquids to making trail mix (solids mixed with solids) and baking breads (separating solids and liquids) for Easton House residents.

"CHILDREN LIVE THERE!?" FURTHERING PERSPECTIVE TAKING

After the winter break, the students were excited to receive a thank-you letter from Easton House residents. One line in the letter astounded them: "The children at Easton House really like the decorations you made." One child exclaimed the sentiment that seemed to echo the group, "*Children* live there?!" Benson could "see their wheels turning." Even though Dewey served the poorest students in the district, mostly from a nearby trailer park, it seemed to be a stretch to the children that their local town had homeless people. Even more unbelievable was the idea that some of those people were *children*. "What might *they* need?" one child in Benson's class asked.

Even though the project was initiated by Mrs. Benson, a more student-driven inquiry flourished from this point on. Homelessness was becoming a less distant idea (and even less scary with the knowledge that there are community supports for those in need) when they considered that they were helping other children. Although they could not solve the problem of poverty, there were some things that the students could do to help. As they considered how people meet their basic needs in the absence of a traditional home, they showed an increased propensity to take perspective and empathize when they thought about the children at Easton House. The students' motivation to continue the project was high, the service-learning project took on "a life of its own," and student-driven inquiry was made possible.

By spring, students independently approached Mrs. Benson to ask what else they could do for Easton House. Although the children wanted to go visit the homeless shelter, they were unable to do so in order to protect the privacy of the residents. Nonetheless, several students expressed concern that the residents might be "getting sick of trail mix," and so they decided to create a survey for Easton House to ask about residents' needs. This is an essential part of good service learning—not presuming what one can do to help the "other," but asking. Indeed, good service is a two-way street of learning, communication, and information sharing. This example shows that service learning can promote empathetic thinking for the "helpers" rather than just feelings of superiority or savior identities. Not only were the students serving the residents; the residents were serving the students by helping them with their academic, civic, and social learning, and developing their sociological imagination.

The ideal of reciprocity models an inquiry approach of asking questions instead of presuming answers. Parker (2003) describes this: "If I am cautious when listening and responding, I will engage carefully so that I am not denying or dismissing the validity of the insider's point of view, nor even appearing to do so" (p. 93). Being a part of an authentic civic relationship (James, Kobe, & Zhao, 2014) involves recognizing the need to attend to interactions of oneself and the other. With Mrs. Benson's help, the students took care to develop thoughtful survey questions for the Easton House residents. Their survey questions included the following: "Would you like us to send more food? If so, would you prefer more trail mix or other food supplies?" and "Do you need anything specific for the children at Easton House?" Some ideas that the children brainstormed included stories written and illustrated by them and gently used toys. The students insisted on including the open-ended question, "Are there other needs you have that we did not mention above?" From that question, they learned that the residents especially appreciated how the students had "handcrafted something for each person." This focus on student-driven inquiry in service learning further promoted their practice in perspective taking, including humility and caution when asking others what they might need and applying new information to make their next decision.

As the previous chapter demonstrated in different ways, a crucial skill in being an active and responsible citizen is seeing the world beyond your own view, imagining others' perspectives, opinions, and experiences. As seen in Chapter 2, this capacity can also be fostered through purposeful read-alouds in which children engage in perspective taking. Benson found another children's book that ignited students' thinking about homelessness, reaching beyond most of their experiences up to that point in their lives. Benson read the students the book, *Sam and the Lucky Money* (Chinn, 1997), in which Sam receives money for a holiday and goes downtown to shop. While downtown, he almost trips over someone's feet. It is a man who is homeless. "Where are his shoes?" Sam asks, as he also begins to learn about homelessness. The children were interested to learn that, in the end, Sam decides to spend his lucky money to help the man. In the book, Sam says to the man, "You can't buy shoes with this . . . but I know you can buy some socks." The students were riveted, said Benson. A more privileged student, Leo, was clearly inspired. One week later, after discussing it with his parents, he brought in $12 that he had saved to go toward supplies for Easton House. He and Benson chose the supplies together. Leo wrote a letter (see Figure 3.1) to Easton House that explained, "I decided to bring some money for supplies. . . . I thought that it would be helpful."

According to Benson, evidence of students' empathetic thinking was happening more regularly. With guidance, students began to make connections between their own families and families that might live at Easton House. Lia, another student, made a card (see Figure 3.2) for the residents of Easton House in which she drew a family and labeled them "you guys." Benson pointed out that the family was the exact configuration of Lia's family, indicating that Lia was able to draw connections between her family and the people living at Easton House, and even to see herself in the "other."

By learning how to engage in perspective taking with homelessness, students also gained a better appreciation of how to take the perspective of their classmates. While the project was ongoing, two 2nd-grade students in Benson's class began an antibullying group called the Fuzzy Buddy Club. This club was formed largely in response to the effects of social exclusion. Without any help or knowledge from Benson, the students explained that their mission as a club was to "stop bullying and spread kindness in our community." At the end of the school year, they bestowed the club's responsibility on two 1st-grade children at a class meeting to ensure that the club would continue. As Mrs. Benson explained this impromptu student-led meeting, she underscored her surprise that she had "no idea they were going to do this" and was touched that they had chosen children who embodied the values of friendship and kindness, regardless of their academic strength or popularity. Mrs. Benson pinpointed how the service-learning project fomented a turning point in her classroom environment and norms, pushing her students' capabilities to empathize and think beyond themselves.

Although we do not suggest that service learning is a cure-all for schools, we value the ways in which it refocuses the curriculum away from individualistic pursuits of high-stakes testing and toward a more collectivist classroom climate. A focus on service can establish norms of caring and thinking of others, including looking at home through another's lens.

CONCLUDING THE PROJECT

Nearly 8 months earlier, to gather baseline data for their unit on habitats, Mrs. Benson asked her students to describe what makes a "home." Throughout the project, Mrs. Benson provided additional opportunities for students to reflect on their growing conception of home through a combination of writing, drawing, and discussion in the classroom. Continuous reflection (occurring before, during, and after a project) is an essential component of service learning that requires participants to

Figure 3.1. Leo's Letter to Easton House

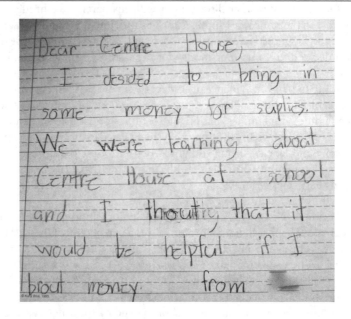

Figure 3.2. Lia's Card

gather data and consider the consequences of their possible actions before action occurs (Eyler, 2002). Student reflections over the course of the project demonstrated how their conceptions of "home" changed from a place defined by material possessions to one where important physical and emotional needs are met. Students moved closer to understanding the basic needs and the human condition.

The class concluded the year by presenting their work with Easton House to the entire school. As the students prepared to present their service work at an All-School Assembly (discussed in Chapter 6), they wrote individual reflections. Reflection is an essential part of service learning (Henry & Breyfogle, 2006) and can take many forms. Benson's students were asked to listen to the lyrics of a song, "My Own Two Hands," and consider, "How did we make a difference? What did we learn?" One child described how they had painted for the shelter, while reporting that the "[w]hole class thought of an idea for [how to help] Easton House." In their final presentation to the entire school, the students shared photos of Easton House and described how there are "actually" homeless people in our own community and what they and others can do to help. By sharing with other students, Benson's students were reinforcing the values of civic action, service learning, and empathy.

In her 2nd year of teaching (in which she retained half of her students, as her 1st-graders became her 2nd-graders), Benson's class continued their service-learning project using their science class time to grow lettuce hydroponically for Easton House residents to eat. Although it may not be possible to have student-led projects or to base the curriculum around civics daily, the results and possibilities for perspective taking, empathy, and building the sociological imagination were evident in Mrs. Benson's class.

LESSONS FOR PRACTICE

There are elements of this project that can be extended to any effort toward establishing mutually beneficial relationships with community partners for service learning while using the project as a center of the academic, civic, and social curriculum. Though it is a lot to ask of teachers to initiate and sustain a large service-learning project while balancing other demands of teaching and assessing, service learning can be a way to apply academic learning to real-world scenarios. And while it can be sticky territory to put students in the role of helper and "others" in the role of the needy, possibly perpetuating the "otherness" of people in need, this example shows that it is possible to do so with an attention to showing empathy and respect for others. Indeed, in any service-learning project, is important to carefully consider how teachers or leaders can thoughtfully promote ethical relations with community partners.

Start small. Especially for 1st-year teachers like Benson, starting with a guest speaker from a possible partner organization can flourish gradually into a large and sustained project. Teachers can begin by introducing a small service project that has clear time parameters and connections to the curriculum. Also, when we suggest starting small, we mean to point out that the children in Benson's class were in the 1st and 2nd grade and that young children should not be dismissed as incapable but rather should be seen as prime for considering the perspective of others and building their capacity for civic action.

Value student voice. Benson enabled and scaffolded young students' voices by making a list of students' ideas regarding how they could help the residents of Easton House. Instead of giving absolute decisionmaking power over to students in their first experiences with service learning (or any civic action project), dialogue and conversation can happen regularly with students on the project's progress to give students increasing amounts of voice in decisionmaking and planning. The teacher can take notes on a whiteboard or chart paper, leading students in committees or deliberation on options. Breaking down the imbalanced wall of power between student and teacher may seem difficult, but we contend that it is an ideal time for students to learn and even maintain a sense of agency in their schooling experience.

Embed civic goals into the core of the curriculum, which can help sustain civic practice in the face of accountability pressures. Service-learning research often speaks of ways to embed standards/curricular goals into community service activities. Doing so gives service learning validity and offers opportunities for rich content learning in schools. It is also important to consider how *civic* goals may be incorporated into core curricular work. In this way, civics and academics can be mutually enhancing.

Focus on inquiry processes to foster authentic, ethical, and experiential service-learning experiences. Instead of presuming they knew the answer, Benson's students asked residents of Easton House what they needed. The teacher and the students were continually wondering what they could do to help. The goals of the project (or any action civics project) were not preset but rather were responsive to the needs of the particular community. The experience should empower and benefit both the community partner and the students. Reciprocity and reflection are key factors in service learning.

Partner with an interested community organization. A partner organization should reflect a societal concern that aligns with the children's interests. It is also important to work with the community partner in conceptualizing appropriate and meaningful service experiences for children. As a leader of service learning, you can let the organization know how you seek to connect the project meaningfully to academic, civic, and social aims. Mrs. Benson described that although this project took time, it resulted in increased student engagement with the curriculum: "I spent several afternoons meeting with our community partners, organizing my own unit plan, and selecting additional resources, such as read-aloud books that I would need to introduce concepts or scaffold student learning. However, the time was well worth the investment, as I believe students were significantly more engaged in writing, math, science, and social studies lessons when we connected our academic work to helping our friends at Easton House."

Educators need not worry if the concern begins as a distant phenomenon (such as homelessness) or a personal one (such as "cutting" in line). The children were most engaged when they could imagine the people, especially children, impacted by their engagement. The *sociological imagination*, the capacity to shift from one perspective to another, is quite apparent in children. Schools can foster a sociological imagination by promoting perspective taking across spaces (geographically) and time (historically). Teachers can ask students (using photos or other visuals) to imagine themselves in others' shoes. Students can interview or survey others to get a grasp on others' perspectives. Seeking to gain the perspective of others can take us deeper and more personally into history, geography, and civic spaces. Perspective taking is a key democratic skill in solving real-world problems, both collectively and reciprocally.

CHAPTER 4

Civic Zines in 5th Grade
Responses to the Call to "Making a Difference"

with Eve Mayes

Ms. Owens sits down cross-legged next to her in a circle of students at the front of the classroom, away from the classroom tables. Some students sit on a couch just behind the circle.

The classroom walls are lined with posters with slogans on them. One reads, "What's going on in our world? Why do I care? Who is affected?" Another reads, "It's not only about the writing. It's also about making a difference." Some of the posters are handmade, made by students. One student-created poster advertises a blood drive organized by two of the boys.

"If you think you can make a difference, raise your hand," Ms. Owens says in a curious tone. Students pause to reflect for a moment, and then hands start to shoot into the air.

Ms. Owens and her students discuss how the students might make a difference in their local community, in their state, and in the world. They talk about current events shown on television news, written about in Internet news sources, and discussed with family.

Ms. Owens then adds, "If you are interested in taking it to the next level, raise your hand. It's optional." Ms. Owens goes onto describe how individuals, like the students themselves, might make a difference in their school, municipality, state, country, world, and so on. One student's hand shoots up into the air. Another student looks down at her lap. Several students look interested but uncertain.

Sitting on the floor with students or on the class couch on a daily basis, Ms. Owens regularly embodies a democratic practice in her 5th-grade classroom, physically positioned alongside the students, asking questions and listening to them speak. Students are invited to participate in democratic deliberation, including forming a list at the beginning of the year based on "what kind of people they hope to be" this academic year, instead of teacher-created class rules or rules at all. Ms. Owens regularly puts civics at the center of her curriculum and teaches the other core subjects through inquiry questions on societal issues. Ms. Owens recently earned "tenure" in her district and is as free-spirited personally as she is as a teacher. She has always adapted the curriculum to make it "hers" and to work for her students. In her 4th year of teaching, she designed an integrated pedagogy called the Civic Zines project. We focus on this project because it demonstrates the ways young people can make a difference and how they can conceptualize that action.

In the previous chapter, we highlighted service learning as a pedagogy that can unite subject areas while also fostering civic engagement. Although service learning is perhaps the most common pedagogy used to unite civic service and academic learning across schools (Billig, 2000) and specifically so at Dewey Elementary, various other civic engagement opportunities exist in the school. These are embedded in curricular practice, cross-age advising groups, weekly schoolwide assemblies run by 5th-grade students, and student participation in schoolwide decisionmaking processes (for example, to modify lunchroom rules). Similarly, Project Citizen (Ponder & Lewis-Ferrell, 2009) and Civic Action Projects (Pope, Stolte, & Cohen, 2011) are similar in inquiring and taking action but do not require the same presentation format (verbal and written) as Ms. Owens's self-created Civic Zines curriculum.

By the 5th grade at Dewey Elementary, students have been well exposed to the idea of civic engagement and been invited to consider how to "make a difference" by taking action in classroom or advisory group settings. Thus, the Civic Zine project exists amid a sociocultural space in which the idea of "making a difference" has been valued and established over time and in various spaces. The purpose of this chapter is to illustrate the Civic Zine project and the students' various responses to the invitation to "make a difference." The project responses simultaneously support and complicate assumptions about civic engagement. We explore three types of responses of four students (two students having a joint and similar response) and discuss their implications for civic engagement in elementary schools.

The concept of "agency" describes the ways in which young people feel they can make a difference in their community. The idea of "making a difference" can also be associated with the cognitive construct of "self-efficacy," defined as the belief that one's actions will result in a certain outcome (Pajares, 1997). We have used the term *efficacy* in other publications (Serriere, 2014). Children's efficacy has been measured in various domains such as athletic, social academic, and so on (e.g., Harter, 1982), generally grounded in cognitive psychology and via surveys. Efficacy has also been categorized in terms of collective and individual efficacy, a conversation we join in this chapter. By using the term "agency" we borrow from these descriptors in this book while utilizing the more sociocultural term *agency*. Our work, however, is grounded in the idea that meaning should be derived within the context of an experience (Dewey, 1938/1998), rather than through a survey.

Similar but larger in scope, the term "civic empowerment" (Levinson, 2012) suggests a larger sphere of impacting social change for citizens. A common and important aspect of these related terms (*civic and political efficacy, agency, civic empowerment*) is a sense that one's actions (individually or with others) can make a difference and positively correlate with the likelihood of various political behaviors, such as voting (Cohen, Vigoda, & Samorly, 2001), becoming politically active

(Abrams & de Moura, 2002), and using informational news media (Newhagen, 1994). The emphasis on test taking in today's sociopolitical educational climate is a major constraint on teaching for civic agency. However, as this chapter shows, when teachers have a clear sense of agency with the curriculum, the teacher's sense of agency entwines with and compounds students' opportunities for experiencing agency.

TEACHING TO "MAKE A DIFFERENCE"

As a citizen temporally and physically "away" from her work at school, Ms. Owens is active in contacting state-level governmental offices regarding educational issues and public school funding (see Chapter 10). She purposefully aims for collaborative, creative, and empowered teaching and citizenship for herself and her students. She describes how the Civic Zine project fits with her hopes for her students:

> I wanted to work to teach the kids [about] civic efficacy and thought current events would be the way to go. I felt that the more they were able to understand all that is going on in the world around them, the more likely they would be to latch on to an issue and want to do something about it.

Ms. Owens seeks to model the ways in which students can make a difference in various spheres—in their classroom, their school, their municipality, their state, their country, and the broader world. She simultaneously recognizes that "making a difference" or taking action should be accompanied by an awareness of the world around them—research and background knowledge on a social issue. She elaborated in an interview:

> Like many other teachers, I wanted to become a teacher in order to try to make a difference in the world. Although I realize I am able to touch the lives of individual children with the hope of somehow making their lives better, richer, etc., I realized that the only true way to make a difference is to teach the kids that they are capable of going out into the world with the hope and efficacy to make a difference.

Her rationale of teaching kids in this way is to make their lives "better, richer, etc." because this is the "only true way to make a difference." Ms. Owens believes that children should have a part in making the world a better place, not just for adults' sake but to make their own lives better. To make her *own* life as a teacher better and richer, she often created her "own thing" to do what she envisioned in the curriculum and also what would fit with her students. Ms. Owens created the Civic Zines project with a colleague after attending a Project Citizen (Center for Civic Education, 1996) teacher workshop. Ms. Owens followed the Project Citizen format in which students collectively identify a public policy problem in their community, select a problem for class study, gather information on the problem for class study, and develop a class portfolio that explains the problem, examines alternative policies, and proposes a public policy and an action plan. The Civic Zine project, described in more detail in the subsequent section, follows a similar format but differs in format and in that Owens has students choose topics individually. The Civic Zine is one example of many in which Ms. Owens creatively and intuitively adapts curriculum in ways that work for her philosophy and practice.

WHAT IS A CIVIC ZINE?

In a letter sent to parents, Ms. Owens described zines as "homemade magazines centered on a current events topic that is of great interest to them." The final product, or artifact, takes the form of either a physical zine, made out of paper and visual materials, or on *Pages* (a word-processing program that allows users to create nice-looking page layouts by Apple) or in an *iBook* (an e-book application by Apple) document, which students can email to her as an attachment. These student-created, multimodal magazines resembled *Discovery Kids* or *National Geographic for Kids* or online magazine subscriptions with moving parts and buttons to press. The written requirements for the zine include an "About the Author" section, a "Dear Reader" section (that is, a first-person letter to the reader that summarizes the zine's contents and purpose), and a list of "credits" (a list of citations and resources). In addition, students are expected to add at least three of the following components as a part of or as a supplement to their zine:

- Organized research notes
- Table of contents
- Poetry
- Statistics or graphs
- Persuasive writing (a piece of writing to convince a person or organization of the topic's importance, advocate for change, or gain support)
- Widgets (videos, links to outside webpages)
- Expository writing that includes interesting facts
- Crossword using relevant vocabulary
- Illustrations that add to the writing

Students are given a checklist with due dates and boxes to tick for subtasks within the zine. Ms. Owens sees this project as integrated across subject areas, and students are encouraged to diversify their sources. Students often engage in mathematical expression by collecting and analyzing data or statistics in graphs or charts. They engage in the arts as they utilize effective or relevant imagery and are required to make a "specially designed cover related to the zine topic made by hand or a combination of handmade and computer-generated artwork." Ms.

Owens mentioned that she seeks ample space for students to demonstrate their understanding using multiple modalities, both artistic and written. Students and parents are provided a rubric for how the zines would be assessed (see Figure 4.1).

Students are also required to give three oral presentations to their class: (1) a "zine defense," in which students state the importance of and rationale of their chosen topic; (2) a "zine update" about halfway through the year, where they inform their classmates and teacher of further information they have found on their topic and action they might be planning; and (3) a final "zine presentation" in which they present their final results and their completed or proposed action. Several students presented their zine topics in All-School Gatherings (a forum described in Chapter 6 in more detail) to gain support and momentum.

Topics chosen by students included blood drives, childhood obesity, and white-nose syndrome in bats. Students gathered their research and wrote their essays in a Google Doc, creating a closed discursive space for the student and teacher to dialogue about the project. Ms. Owens communicated regularly with parents about the project through formal letters and emails, so parents could ask questions and discuss the project with their children. In several instances, parents did their own research with their children and played an active role in supporting their children's interests.

Ms. Owens believes that students' civic writing can be *meaningful* and *authentic*. It is important for students to select a topic that *they* consider important and interesting. The students are positioned as having the capacity to write to inform a specific audience for the purpose of solving real-world problems. Students responded in multiple ways to the project, from high levels of interest and engagement to "just getting it done" like any other assignment. Notably, Ms. Owens did not assign a grade on the civic action, or "making a difference" as she called it, portion of their zine projects. In spite of or despite a grade as an extrinsic motivator, a number of students took action that went beyond the scope of the assessment. Two male students, Josh and J.D., working with the Red Cross, organized a blood drive in which more than 90 adults in the school community gave blood. One student, Anna Lisa, set up a container where she attempted to collect money for a local organization resisting hydraulic fracking. Another student, Emma, saw the project merely as another assignment to complete and finish as quickly as possible without engaging in actively trying to "making a difference." In the next three sections, we discuss these students and three variations on agency or "making a difference" expressed through this project by the students: *instrumental agency*, *consumer agency*, and *collective agency*.

INSTRUMENTAL AGENCY

Emma was a quiet, highly motivated, and procedurally driven student in Ms. Owens's classroom. In comparison to most of her fellow students, she had less of a belief that she could impact change on her chosen issue of global warming, saying

Figure 4.1. Civic Zines Assessment

CURRENT EVENT ZINE PROJECT
A MULTIGENRE WRITING PROJECT

Dear Families,

Our 5th-graders are about to embark on a fun writing adventure, which will require about 5 months of diligent research and writing work. They have begun to make homemade magazines centered on a current events topic that is of great interest to them. The following information will provide you with specific details and deadlines for various parts of the zine. **The completed zine is due on MONDAY, APRIL 16, 2012.**

DUE NOVEMBER 29

- Zine Topic Defense
- Students will come to school prepared with information to explain their zine topic choice.

DUE JANUARY 16

(Please refer to the attached rubric for specific expectations.)

- About the Author (final version in Google Docs)
- Dear Reader (final version in Google Docs)
- Subject will be thoroughly researched and notes organized (students are responsible for turning in their notes at the end of the assignment)
- Informational writing will be organized using a graphic organizer
- Informational writing rough draft (handwritten)

DUE FEBRUARY 6

(Please refer to the attached rubric for specific expectations.)

- Informational writing (final version in Google Docs)
- Persuasive writing graphic organizer complete
- Persuasive writing rough draft (handwritten)
- Plot map for narrative story (include five elements of a plot)

DUE MARCH 2

(Please refer to the attached rubric for specific expectations.)

- Persuasive writing (final version in Google Docs)
- Narrative writing plot map
- Narrative writing rough draft (handwritten)

DUE MARCH 9

- Completed cover (a specially designed cover related to the zine topic made by hand or a combination of handmade and computer-generated artwork).

DUE MARCH 30

(Please refer to the attached rubric for specific expectations.)

- Narrative writing (final version in Google Docs)
- *DUE IN THE COMPLETED ZINE ON MONDAY, APRIL 16*

(Please refer to the attached rubric for specific expectations.)

Other types of writing (choose three):

- Organized research notes (not to be included in the zine)
- Table of Contents
- Acrostic poems

(continued)

Figure 4.1. Civic Zines Assessment *(continued)*

- Poetry
- Letter
- Crossword
- Interesting facts
- Optional illustration if it adds to the writing
- Other

All written pieces will be fully revised and edited. Prior to writing the final, published piece, each must go through a student/teacher conference and peer editing. Also, this project will be completed between home and school. The kids are very familiar with Google Docs and have complete access to their work at home and at school. Of course, they need to be responsible for bringing their handwritten or printed notes back and forth. Much of the writing and planning will be done in school. Periodically, homework will include parts of this project. Overall, this project will look like a magazine, similar to *Discovery Kids* or *National Geographic for Kids*. We will share examples and provide support for all genres of writing.

Please let us know if you have any questions or comments!

Sincerely, [names deleted]

ZINE RUBRIC

	4	3	2	1
Appearance—visual presentation of information	Information and illustrations are well organized visually, i.e., not cluttered or too far apart. Color is used effectively.	Information and illustrations are mostly well organized visually, i.e., slightly cluttered or too far apart. Color is used mostly effectively.	Information and illustrations are somewhat well organized visually, i.e., somewhat cluttered or too far apart. Color is used somewhat effectively.	Information and illustrations are not well organized visually, i.e., very cluttered or too far apart. Color is not used at all or effectively.
Illustrations—appropriateness to subject matter and writing	The illustrations directly relate to and enhance the writing.	The illustrations mostly relate to and enhance the writing.	The illustrations somewhat relate to and enhance the writing.	The illustrations do not directly relate to or enhance the writing.
Readability—Text is large enough to see and legibly written, headers are bold and larger than text	Text is large enough to see and legibly written or typed in an easy-to-read font; headers are bold and larger than text.	Text is mostly large enough to see and legibly written; headers are bold and larger than text.	Text is difficult to see and somewhat legible; headers are not bold or larger than text.	Text is illegible and headers are nonexistent.
Zine includes required written pieces and illustrations	Zine includes at least 6 pieces of writing and 3 or more illustrations, maps, diagrams, and so on.	Zine includes at least 4 pieces of writing and 3 or more illustrations, maps, diagrams, and so on.	Zine includes at least 3 pieces of writing and 2 or more illustrations, maps, diagrams, and so on.	Zine includes fewer than 2 pieces of writing and 1 illustration, map, diagram, and so on.

that her topic was "too big." Emma had emigrated from China 2 years prior to this project, and she spoke of her parents mostly in terms of them encouraging her to get good grades, achieve in school, and complete her homework. In the "About the Author" section of her zine, Emma described herself as "a nice, funny quiet person who wants to help people make friends." Emma chose global warming as her zine topic in a spur-of-the-moment decision made when the teacher asked about her topic in a whole-class setting. Unlike many students who expressed positive articulation of the experience, Emma described sharing her zine topic as follows:

> [Ms. Owens] just asked everyone what their project was. And at the end I was the last one to pick a topic. And at the end I started to panic and then climate change just suddenly got into my mind.

Emma's description of her emotions in this situation suggests that she is afraid of being positioned in front of her peers as lacking interest in civic issues, or perhaps being academically disorganized. Emma repeated on several occasions that global warning "just popped into my mind" and that she chose the topic because "I couldn't think of anything else." Emma expressed reservations about "making a difference" throughout the project, preferring to talk about the zine checklist artifact and task completion: "I don't really like making a difference. I just think that just writing and getting over with it is better."

Emma's logic of "getting it over with" centered on a key artifact of productivity and getting the project done: the Zine Checklist. The Zine Checklist included elements described above in checklist form, made by Ms. Owens for students' reference as they worked to complete the required elements. Whenever a member of our research team asked how her project was going (in informal check-ins and interviews), Emma referred to the Zine Checklist and described her progress in relation to the completion of the project's tasks. When we asked her to describe her feelings about the project during the first interview, Emma spoke about finishing the work rather than making a difference:

> I felt pretty proud [when I finished my zine defense] . . . because I like had to make all these perfect round circles and then draw all these bars and it's pretty hard to fit all those words. . . . Every time I tick off something I think, "Yes, I'm finished" and I immediately go on to the next thing.

Rather than seeing the project in terms of positive emotion of being empowered and excited to "make a difference" like many other students did, Emma used another metaphor to describe how she would feel when her zine was completed:

> I will feel like there's a ton, like a ball that weighs a ton [she holds her hands to her neck, miming that there is a ball and chain around it], off my shoulder [drops her hands to her sides, miming it falling off]. If I get the zine off my list, then there will be a lot less to worry about.

Emma's persistence in redirecting conversations with the researcher back to the checklist was quite striking, considering how the interview questions were interactively positioning her to speak about "making a difference." In one informal conversation, when one of the researchers asked Emma whether she agreed with a classroom poster artifact's slogan, "It's not only about good writing, it's about making a difference," Emma responded:

> Well, I don't really like making a difference. I just think that just writing and getting over with it is better—I don't really like doing this project since you have to do lots of projects and they're due at certain times.

Emma distanced herself from the notion of "making a difference," preferring to focus on the project completion, exemplified and driven by her fixation on the zine checklist. To Emma, the zine project was a way to show her productivity and ability to accomplish tasks. We see Emma's use of instrumentalist logic as a way in which she conceptualized making a difference in society. Such a version of a citizen as a producer or productive citizen for the future is supported by much of the current national educational rhetoric of high-stakes testing, individualism, and competition. However, the element of Emma's culture is important to untangle carefully. One may surmise that her fixation with the right answer is a result of the fact that she is an Asian American and is using a model-minority framework to analyze these data. However, it has been noted that this lens homogenizes Asian Americans as a fixed "other." Alternatively, one could see Emma's response to the project with a deficit lens, noting that she lacks familiarly or ease with Western progressive pedagogies and prefers to focus on one right answer. However, either of these interpretations is overly deterministic of Emma's culture and discounts the purposeful and myriad choices Emma made during the project.

CONSUMER AGENCY

In contrast to Emma, Anna Lisa displayed a high level of belief in her ability to make a difference and specifically through funneling economic help to a cause. She investigated the environmental impact of hydraulic fracking drilling in the local community. In her zine defense at the end of the project, she described the issue as follows:

> Have you ever heard of Marcellus Shale? It is a huge cavern way underground filled to the brim with natural gas. It's the largest known rock formation filled with the gas in the country, maybe even the continent. Natural gas is kind of hard to get your hands on, and people could get rich by selling it for energy. Naturally, tons of companies are coming to drill for gas, and that's causing all kinds of problems.

Anna Lisa expressed her concern for the impact of fracking on the community's health in an interview: "This [issue] is affecting too many people. I want to help them because it's in my area and people could get sick." In addition to the multimodal zone component that would be formally assessed and shared, her main goal for her project (beyond the multimodal zine component that was being formally assessed) was to raise money for the Sierra Club to supply clean water tanks for community members whose water supplies were contaminated by the fracking. At every point in the project, Anna Lisa was optimistic about her project. After graduating to middle school, she contacted Ms. Owens to see if another student would like to continue her project and fundraising drive.

In addition to the zine itself, Anna Lisa created another artifact as part of the project: a collection container made out of a plastic ice cream carton with a hole cut in the top and a sign imploring visitors at Dewey to "HELP GET CLEAN WATER TO FAMILIES IMPACTED BY FRACKING!" Anna Lisa's dialogue of the collection container throughout and after the project indicated how she was making meaning of the discourses around civic agency. With similar zeal for a presentation to the entire school and the zine itself, Anna Lisa focused on donations to the collection container as a source of motivation and progress in her work. She explained this goal in an interview:

> I want to set up a drive so people can donate money in this school. They can donate money and we'll give it to [a local philanthropic organization]. [The organization] will fill these huge water tanks in houses that will allow them (people whose water is polluted from fracking) to take showers without having to open their windows for ventilation to get out the toxic fumes.

Earlier in the process, she also described how her presentation and communication skills would be important in inspire people to donate or do something about the issue:

> I'm going to explain what fracking is. . . . I'm going to say people's water is disgusting because fracking is pumping chemicals into it and stuff. I set up a drive, and please donate money to it so we can help people get clean water that they can use.

Anna Lisa recognized that part of awareness-raising involves evoking an emotional response from people and is necessary to move people to donate: "Maybe if enough people get to feel this way, maybe they can help the people who already know and make a change, because so many people say, this is ridiculous." She spoke directly about how she wanted to make people feel in order for them to donate.

Anna Lisa clarified that for her, the issue was not that companies wanted to "get rich" by selling gas for energy, but rather the environment-harming methods utilized in hydraulic fracking:

I think that they're doing this because [the area] is just filled with natural gas, and they can make millions of dollars selling that gas for energy and sending it overseas to like Russia. I think . . . they think that's a good way to get money, and so they come and drill. I don't think there's anything wrong with that; I just think that the way they're doing it is bad.

Following her logic, individual citizens can also use money to reallocate monies, therefore reducing the negative actions of companies, though it is not "wrong" in itself for companies to make large profits.

At Dewey Elementary, collection containers were often placed in the school atrium by groups or classrooms, such as for Toys for Tots and food and supplies for the local animal shelter. Anna Lisa displayed her collection container with a sign on it in the school's atrium. By participating in this aspect of Dewey civic culture as an individual, Anna Lisa positioned herself with agency in her school. In telling her teachers and peers about the container during a schoolwide assembly and our research team about the container during our visits, Anna Lisa participated in a civic identity that was both recognizable and praised at the school. From our data, students, teachers, and administration responded positively to her actions as citizen with agency. In the context of Dewey Elementary, her placement of the collection container in a school corridor was seen as a positive act rather than a disruptive one, as it may be seen in other schools. These specific cultural norms and practices at Dewey Elementary support, celebrate, and embed civic engagement within its culture.

Anna Lisa explained that her ability to make a difference had been limited by her inability to distribute her zine: "I can't make hundreds of copies of this and give them out." She said, "I think learning about it, spreading the word and doing a little drive that I've set up is best and is the way that I'm making a difference." Still, a few months into becoming a student at her new middle school, Anna Lisa sent an email to Ms. Owens expressing her desire to continue the fracking work: "I was hoping to continue my fracking drive even though I am not at [Dewey Elementary] anymore. I will make a container at some point. Maybe your new class would like to help with it?" This email could be interpreted as Anna Lisa coming to increasingly identify with "making a difference," or longing for a space in which she felt she could make a difference.

Anna Lisa's process of being a civic agent did not neatly align with the social justice visions of Ms. Owens. Instead, Anna Lisa's articulation of her civic agency was informed by the idea of *consumer citizenship*. During an interview discussion with one researcher, discussing how a person might hypothetically make a difference in their life, Anna Lisa said, "You can make a difference about anything." She then pointed to the peacock feathers dyed orange that the researcher was wearing to elaborate on her understanding of the ends of making a difference:

I love your earrings; I've been thinking they're really cool—and maybe if they only came in orange, I could make a difference because I could . . . [go]

to the company and [say], "Is orange really the only color you have? They look great but they would also look good in other colors."

In this response, Anna Lisa conflated social justice notions of making a difference and more individualistic understandings of consumer voice.

For Anna Lisa, making a difference entails presenting a cause with a collection container and then collecting donations for it. Her ideas about citizenship mirror the paradoxical term of a "citizen-consumer hybrid" (Johnston, 2008; Jubas, 2007). The concept highlights underlying ideological tensions and contradictions between being the "citizen" and the seemingly more collectively responsible locus for the common good (cf. Johnston, 2008; Mol, 2009). In the United States particularly, the expression "your dollar is your vote" or "dollar voting" exemplifies a notion of consumer citizenship that implies that through their actions as consumers citizens have the agency to impact production and the economy. Because Ms. Owens was a proponent of social change, and fundraising was seen at Dewey as a common mode for addressing social ills, Anna Lisa created a response that was directly related to her immediate sociocultural context but also drew from larger discourses about how to make a difference through monetary means.

COLLECTIVE AGENCY

Two other students, the last two student responses we will describe in this chapter, in Ms. Owens's class, Josh and J.D., separately chose the topic of blood shortages. They later paired the taking action or "making a difference" portion of their project by hosting a blood drive in their school's gymnasium. For the written portion of their zine, they shared resources and ideas, even while writing their zines as distinctly unique and separate documents. Josh explained, "We wanted to make them different as much as possible so you could read both and still get different information from both." The culminating blood drive was a clear joint effort and "visible victory" (McLaughlin, 1993) that surprised both of the boys based on their initial project goals. In this section, we describe the evolution of the boys' process and the importance of collective support in their success.

Josh is an expressive, extroverted, and clever 5th-grade student who wants to educate his classmates and community about the importance of blood donation. At the onset of the project, Josh expressed his interest in blood donation in an individual interview: "I care about this topic because it can save lives and I have relatives that have had their lives saved. Also, many more people are needed to donate blood because we are low on supplies." Even though Josh expressed a personal interest in his topic, he was apprehensive about the magnitude of work required to complete the zine project requirements. He also initially questioned the likelihood that his project would make a difference. He casually stated, "I'll maybe convince some people to donate" when asked early on what he hoped to accomplish in terms of "making a difference."

The other student, J. D., is a comical and procedurally oriented 5th-grade student who decided to work with Josh because they coincidentally shared an interest in blood donation. Despite initial evidence that J. D. might not be completely engaged or very interested in the project as he socialized with various friends during zine work time, he demonstrated sincere interest in the topic when asked about it one-on-one. He explained first that "I have a friend who needed a blood transfusion" and then said he had seen signs for blood drive competitions in the nearby university where his dad works and they "seemed fun." At the onset of the project, he explained, he didn't have any goals except "just finishing the zine," much like Emma in the first case. Then, his interest seemed to build as he explained, "I went to the American Red Cross (with Josh) and got some information about who needs blood and why they need blood, and how often they might need it." Still, his belief that he would actually do a blood drive was uncertain at that point. When asked what he thought his chances were that he would meet his goal of "making a difference" by creating a blood drive, he replied, "I don't know, about 50/50, because I still have to finish our zine." He clarified how his hopes to make a difference grew when he and Josh "got thinking" about how every little town should have a blood drive. According to J. D., they started working and brainstorming together and the ideas for a blood drive at Dewey Elementary took clearer shape.

Josh and J. D.'s project was also one of the two projects featured in a visit to Mrs. Benson's 1st-/2nd-grade class (see chapter three) to tell the students there about two of their Civic Zines projects. Benson's 1st-/2nd-grade class voted to take on the blood drive as a joint service project with Owen's 5th grade class. Following a Project Citizen protocol, the younger students simultaneously researched the issue of blood drives and proposed this blood drive as a way to help the school community. This was a burgeoning moment in J. D. and Josh's project plans and their conception of "making a difference," which now included helping younger students "catch on." J. D. explained:

> We started a project with kids down in 1st and 2nd grade and so that's why Project Citizen is what it is. They had to vote on two topics. One was blood drives, so they picked blood drives. Right there, my teacher thought that's a perfect opportunity so they can catch on.

J. D. and Josh were now not only planning a blood drive, but they were serving as a model to younger students at Dewey. J. D. and Josh became stewards of civic engagement and quite well known within their school for this project. The collective support working across classrooms and into the school's larger community further buoyed the blood drive project.

As the details, plans, and campaign for the blood drive developed, the boys were interviewed on a local radio station. In their radio spot, the boys encouraged the pubic to come to Dewey Elementary and donate:

> *Josh:* Did you know that every two seconds a person needs blood? Come
> down to "Dewey" Elementary on Thursday, May 7th, for our blood drive!

J. D.: If you're at least 16 and haven't donated in the last 30 days, you can
donate! Refreshments will also be handed out.
[Simultaneously and with other children]: Please donate! Every life is
important!

Their efforts of advertising and partnering paid off because the blood drive's
sign up was full several days before the event. On the day of the event, Josh was
dressed in costume as a drop of blood and welcomed community members on the
way in. Other children stood with clipboards, welcoming adults and checking their
appointment time. Adults facilitated the children's work. When a donor was called
to the donation area, a Dewey child (usually a 5th grader) escorted them. After the
blood donation, the Dewey child led the adult by the elbow toward the snack and
drink area. Dewey teachers, children, and parents donated all snacks and drinks.
The Dewey community deemed the blood drive a huge success.

J. D. was quite aware that his ability to succeed in making a difference was a
result of the collective buy-in for his project. When asked if he believed he could
make a difference, J. D. responded, "Yes . . . 'cause I have friends that help me." He
later clarified that he believes he probably could make a difference without friends
but that "they make it easier and funner [*sic*] to do." The collective support made
it more likely that he would succeed. J. D. added that he was most successful in his
work by "getting quiet" because he could then type faster and get work done, as
compared to his usual more social modus. He then came back to his partnership
with Josh to clarify another idea that helped him succeed: "checking in with Josh.
. . . If I had to work by myself, it'd be a little bit harder."

Both boys expressed their surprise in having such clear success in making
a difference. Josh explained, "I thought like, 'Oh yeah, I'll maybe convince some
people to go donate. That's what I'm going to do.' Then we actually have a blood
drive that's happening. That's just really cool." He continued with more gusto, addressing the perception that people think kids cannot make a difference:

I know I can make a difference and it makes me kind of angry that people
don't think I can make a difference because I've been working hard on this
and people are like, "Oh you can't make a difference; you're just a kid." So
I'm like, "Okay. You'll see."

We then asked Josh if he believed he can make a difference. He responded
enthusiastically, "Yes!" and added, "We now have the blood drive happening here.
I think that's making a huge difference." He added that this belief grew over time:

Just over time knowing that I'm making a difference with this means that
if you really want to do something and you just set your mind to it and you
just keep working, I feel like you could make a difference on anything.

Although Josh did not articulate as precisely as J. D. did the impact of collective support, he pointed to the social expectation to make a difference in the

Dewey community: "So I am making a difference, so nobody can say now that my zine is not making a difference because we are making a difference by having the blood drive here." Ms. Owens wanted her students to "make a difference," but the social expectation was not only created by her.

CONSIDERING YOUNG PEOPLE AS INDIVIDUAL AGENTS OF SOCIAL CHANGE

Although instrumental, consumer, and collective agency are three responses with their own unique logic and ideas about citizenship, we recognize that these descriptions are both overlapping and incomplete. Consumer agency cannot occur without the logics of instrumentalism and collective support. The collective agent must rely on instrumental agency to get through the many tasks of completing a large-scale project like a blood drive. Enacting citizenship as social justice, as in Westheimer and Kahne's (2004) justice-oriented citizen, also involves enacting individual (personally-responsible) and participant citizenship skills that may eventually work to impact justice.

The rituals, routines, artifacts, and discourse around Dewey Elementary supported the idea that young people can and should make a difference in society. This process begins at an early age as teachers foster students who become knowledgeable and socially aware about the communities surrounding them. Through this project, teachers can support meaningful integration of subject areas and foster children's ability to make changes in society. This also involves support and allowance for (1) high levels of student choice within the project and (2) multiple responses to acceptable modes for "making a difference."

Regardless of teacher framing, not all students (or parents) will buy into the idea that kids can or should make a societal difference in elementary school. Students like Emma and her parents may not fit into the dominant "democratic" discourse at Dewey and may respond in more traditional, task-driven ways. This case raises the question of how to define successful civic engagement, and if becoming a change agent is an appropriate goal for all students. According to Ms. Owens's beliefs, educators should stick to our beliefs regardless of others' visions for education. She explained her rationale: "I don't want them (her students) to just get through school. I want school to be something that's helping them. . . ." She then cited research that "universities are feeling like the students that are coming to them now don't know how to think. . . . They know how to take a test, but they don't know how to process the information. If you have professors from Harvard saying these kids have 4.3 GPAs, how? We don't even understand how they've achieved that. I don't want that for my students." Ms. Owens explained that it was not just about making time in the school day for students to do "what they want;" she clarified her commitment to making that time "personally meaningful" to her students.

Understanding the diverse reactions to invitations to make a difference might be as important as framing widely and specifically what counts as making a difference. The teacher skill involved in the zine project involves supporting and being knowledgeable about various modes of making a difference from awareness raising, fundraising, campaigning, or letter writing, which Ms. Owens did as best as she could. Another complication with so much autonomy and choice in a project like the Civic Zines is that not all students have the kind of collective support and knowledge from a group project that J. D. and Josh enjoyed. We recognize that it takes a high level of teacher skill to support many individual students' projects toward various modes of success. Children like Anna Lisa might use the only modes of making a difference they know of, such as collection containers, whereas children like Emma, who are relatively new to the school and come from another country, might never have been exposed to the concept of making a difference, or even the idea of collection cans.

Students' choices in making a difference are far from apolitical. As teachers, it is important to support diverse responses with political implications across the spectrum. Doing so fosters the kind of rich discourse that is necessary not only in a democracy but for students to experience civic life fully. Though Anna Lisa's disdain for fracking might be perceived as privileged by a student whose family livelihood depends on the natural gas industry, we see such engagement with a diversity of opinions and interests as a rich and crucial part of learning to live in a diverse democratic society.

LESSONS FOR PRACTICE

Encourage divergent thinking. In an era of accountability and focus on one correct and testable answer, the ability to choose, decide, evaluate, and make a critical case for a social need is vital. The zine project is a model of the ways in which schools can meet some necessary competencies for students (such as expository, narrative, and persuasive writing) while also encouraging a critical awareness and interest in social, environmental, and civic issues around them. This project shows the range of individual responses from the invitation of one project.

Seek divergent voices. The accountability era presumes that knowledge and information is static and can be memorized. This view of knowledge could promote a monoculture while leaving out minority and diverse students' experiences (Paris, 2012). Although encouraging students' voices (stories, opinions, or personal issues) cannot be taken for granted, leveraging a platform for engagement may allow underprivileged students to participate politically and civically in ways that are authentic and personally meaningful, rather than reifying (i.e., Schultz 2008). To close the civic achievement gap and avoid further alienating diverse student populations (Levinson, 2010), teachers must consider students' diverse racial, ethnic, and socioeconomic backgrounds in framing civic participation with, to, and for students. In particular, teachers of civics can support different students' participation and recognize their diverse strengths.

Offer choice and supports. When students choose their own individual civic action projects, they are encouraged to develop their own interests and opinions in the world, which detracts from creating collective civic action projects. The likelihood of "making a difference" increases with the supports of a group project, as seen here when we contrast J. D. and Josh's project with Emma's or Anna Lisa's. We will also discuss the power of collective civic action when discussing the student-initiated work of the "Salad Girls" (described in Chapter 8). Civic engagements in the elementary years can and should support projects initiated by students and teachers, and taken on both individually and collectively.

Create spaces for engagement. Last, it is important to attend to creating supportive spaces for civic engagement. Some of these supports we have found to be meaningful for sustained civic action include spaces for collaboration and feedback and spaces for visible victories. At the schoolwide level, students like Anna Lisa utilized the space of the school atrium to engage in the creation of civic action, an opportunity that is openly available to all students and groups. Students like Anna Lisa, J. D., and Josh also utilized the school space of the All-School Assemblies to garner support for their project.

In conclusion, although teachers who ask their students to write for purposes of social change may be rare, this example shows that speaking, writing, and researching can be *meaningful*, *authentic*, and *supportive* of civic engagement in students' early years. To become citizens who impact social change, young people must first be positioned as having the capacity to influence change, to write and speak to inform a specific audience for the purpose of solving real-world problems. Students respond with the rich and diverse lenses they bring to school rather than in homogenous or obedient ways.

Writing a School Constitution
Representative Democracy in Action

by Teacher Stacey Benson & Principal Shannon

A core philosophy of our school is to provide a "laboratory" in which students can live and learn democracy in action. As a learning community, we continually seek to help students develop the skills necessary for meaningful participation in our democracy. To engage in an understanding of representative democracy, we designed a long-term, schoolwide learning experience in which all students in grades K–5 could develop a Dewey Elementary School Constitution. The purpose was to create an authentic and stimulating learning experience that would prepare students for the challenges of adult life and citizenship. Through this inquiry-based process, Dewey teachers worked with students to engage in collaborative discussions with diverse partners, construct arguments with evidence and reasoning, make sense of problems and persevere in solving them, and analyze America's founding documents (National Governors Association, 2014).

The process of writing a school constitution gave students an opportunity to engage meaningfully in democratic practices and to develop an understanding of the need for representative government. By wrestling with authentic questions of "self-government," students were able to practice the important citizenship skills of asking questions, listening for understanding, seeking alternative viewpoints, disagreeing constructively, and building consensus within a group. Within the safety of our learning community, students were approximating the time-consuming—and often messy—democratic process and learning to work together as citizens.

At the beginning of every school year at Dewey, it is the custom of each teacher to convene his/her class and to invite his/her students to participate in establishing guidelines for behavior and citizenship in the classroom. In 2012–2013, however, we began the school year by taking this process a step further: All PFE students attended a series of eight All-School Assemblies throughout the first 2 weeks of school, during which classes shared their visions for an ideal school/learning community with one another. Although these meetings generated many important ideas for the year ahead, they also evoked some feelings of frustration and boredom among students. Through this process, many students came to recognize the difficulty of sharing ideas and solving problems in a large community using direct democracy. This experience set the stage on which we launched a yearlong project to write a PFE Constitution through representative democracy and a Constitutional Convention.

Students elected classroom representatives, or delegates, from among their peers to represent them at a PFE Constitutional Convention. We began the election process by providing teachers with lesson ideas that would help students explore representative democracy as a way to share ideas and create a unified vision for our school. These lessons included age-appropriate methods for helping students identify desirable qualities for classroom representatives and evaluate potential candidates based on those qualities. For example, in grades K–2, students examined their favorite characters from children's literature (e.g., Curious George, Olivia) to evaluate whether these characters would make good classroom representatives. In grades 3–5, students examined the Electoral College system, engaged in opinion writing to explain the desirable qualities of classroom representatives, and delivered speeches in support of various candidates. Students then voted by secret ballot for the classmate(s) who would best represent their classroom at a Constitutional Convention. Each class tallied its votes to determine its elected representative and an alternate.

Beginning a few weeks after the election, representatives and alternates were released from their classrooms for two afternoons to attend the PFE Constitutional Convention. Given that the representatives and alternates ranged in grade level from kindergarten through grade 5, we began the first meeting of the convention by introducing/activating students' prior knowledge about the meaning of the word *constitution*. Students shared their ideas and knowledge and then listened to the words of the Preamble to the U.S. Constitution as sung by children (Wilbur, 2011). Following the song, we revisited our ideas about the purpose of a "Constitution" and discussed the concepts of "rights" and "responsibilities." Students then engaged in a series of activities to sort all of the ideas generated by "the people" through the town-hall meetings into two groups: ideas about "rights" and ideas about "responsibilities." Before Day 1 of the Constitutional Convention was adjourned, students established three working committees that would convene at the next meeting: a committee to write the Preamble, a committee to revise and edit the rights and responsibilities, and a committee to illustrate the Constitution in order to make it accessible to our youngest citizens.

At the second meeting of our Constitutional Convention, representatives and alternates began meeting in their working committees to create the components of our document. The Preamble committee analyzed the text of the Preamble to the U.S. Constitution and used it as a model for the structure and language of a PFE Preamble. The Rights and Responsibilities committee used the "Dotmocracy" process created by Jason Diceman (2013) to select the most important items in each category and then crafted language to communicate the ideas of "the people" in short, powerful sentences. The Illustration committee took the revised rights and responsibilities and reproduced them with colorful illustrations that kindergarten and primary students would understand. At the end of the afternoon of Day 2, all representatives and alternates reconvened to share their work, compile it into a draft Constitution, and vote to approve the draft.

In the month following the second meeting of the Constitutional Convention, classroom representatives and alternates brought the physical draft of the Constitution to their classrooms and shared information about their process and the document with the classmates whom they had represented. Fifth-grade representatives assisted the representatives from kindergarten and primary classrooms by visiting their classrooms and helping the younger representatives explain the document and answer questions from their peers. Finally, after the draft PFE Constitution had traveled to every classroom, an All-School Assembly was held at which all PFE students and staff had the opportunity to vote to ratify the Constitution. The final, ratified document now hangs in a prominent location in our school atrium, with copies posted in all classrooms.

Part II

SCHOOLS AS SITES FOR CIVIC ENGAGEMENT

While Part I focused on classroom-based civic engagement, the chapters in this part focus on schoolwide civic engagement. The value of having structures that can enable civic action and provide spaces for student voice has been discussed in previous research. Such structures include addressing the high-pressured school climate related to student examinations and homework pressures and subsequent mental stress for students (Galloway, Pope, & Osberg, 2007; Mitra, 2001), whole-school reform and evaluation of assessment policies (Yonezawa & Jones, 2007), and visioning and strategic planning for the future (Eccles & Gootman, 2002; Zeldin, 2004). In Part II, we especially consider how leadership and school structures foster civic engagement. We explore how Dewey aligns with research on the impact of administrative and teacher leadership on school change (Brezicha, Bergmark, & Mitra, 2015; Louis, Marks, & Kruse, 1996; Spillane, Halverson, & Diamond, 2001) and especially involving young people in change processes (Mitra, 2004; Mitra, Serriere, & Stoicovy, 2012). The structures and routines of Dewey also helped promote and protect the vision of a school as a hub of civic engagement. They also fostered horizontal ties to the community-based civic engagement, which we will discuss in Part III.

Dewey leadership values the development of spaces and programs in which students actively learn about and through their community using tools of inquiry and democratic principles to create "meaningful learner engagement" for each child. Looking across these chapters, we can see that this kind of "meaningful learner engagement" at Dewey builds on the principles of critical inquiry, democracy and student voice, community, and environmental stewardship for the purpose of fostering. This vision was articulated explicitly in a diagram that Principal Shannon shared widely within the school and during her many meetings outside of school walls (see Figure II.1 for the diagram and further definition of terms). She developed this vision collaboratively with teachers at the school. The overarching mission statement of Dewey states: "A caring community of learners connecting our learning spaces to the world outside."

Figure II.1. Caring Community Diagram

A caring community of learners connecting our learning to the world outside.

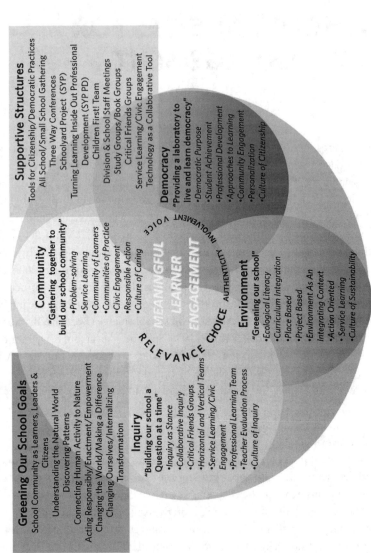

Greening Our School Goals
School Community as Learners, Leaders & Citizens
Understanding the Natural World
Discovering Patterns
Connecting Human Activity to Nature
Acting Responsibly/Enactment/Empowerment
Changing the World/Making a Difference
Changing Ourselves/Internalizing Transformation

Supportive Structures
Tools for Citizenship/Democratic Practices
All School/Small School Gathering
Three Way Conferences
Schoolyard Project (SYP)
Turning Learning Inside Out Professional Development (SYP PD)
Children First! Team
Division & School Staff Meetings
Study Groups/Book Groups
Critical Friends Groups
Service Learning/Civic Engagement
Technology as a Collaborative Tool

Community
"Gathering together to build our school community"
• Problem-solving
• Service Learning
• Community of Learners
• Communities of Practice
• Civic Engagement
• Responsible Action
• Culture of Caring

Democracy
"Providing a laboratory to live and learn democracy"
• Democratic Purpose
• Student Achievement
• Professional Development
• Approaches to Learning
• Community Engagement
• Personalization
• Culture of Citizenship

Inquiry
"Building our school a Question at a time"
• Inquiry as Stance
• Collaborative Inquiry
• Critical Friends Groups
• Horizontal and Vertical Teams
• Service Learning/Civic Engagement
• Professional Learning Team
• Teacher Evaluation Process
• Culture of Inquiry

Environment
"Greening our school"
• Ecological Literacy
• Curriculum Integration
• Place Based
• Project Based
• Environment As An Integrating Context
• Action Oriented
• Service Learning
• Culture of Sustainability

MEANINGFUL LEARNER ENGAGEMENT
INVOLVEMENT VOICE
AUTHENTICITY CHOICE
RELEVANCE

Because this section is about the structures and process that reach the entire school, we focus directly on Principal Shannon's leadership in the school. Shannon's 30-plus years of experience in schools, including more than 25 years at Dewey, shone through a steady focus on civic engagement. At Dewey, Shannon cast her role as a "lead learner" in the school, rather than as a principal to signal her equal with others in the school and participation in the inquiry learning process. She exhibited persistence and dedication to her vision. A quiet leader, Shannon usually shunned the spotlight and preferred to have teachers make presentations. She took care to involve other teachers in building these initiatives and in seeking input on next steps. Yet there is no denying Shannon's influence clearly shaped the vision of the school.

Teacher leadership at Dewey is strong. According to a grant written by Principal Shannon, "The Dewey professional staff may be best described as having a high commitment to innovation, student achievement, and teacher autonomy." As the largest elementary professional staff in its district, Dewey's teachers included a broad range of career and teaching experiences. A conscious effort was made by Principal Shannon to hire teachers at all stages of their career. Twenty percent (20%) of the teachers chose teaching as a second career and another 20% first worked at Dewey as yearlong interns while finishing certification programs at a local university.

Building on the foundation of a visionary principal and strong teacher leadership, a cross-cutting theme in this section is the idea that *vision must balance teacher voice/buy-in with maintaining the integrity of the vision of the school.* While Shannon viewed flexibility as important, she also modeled a strong vision for the school and an expectation that teachers would work under the school's philosophy. Fostering a space for civic engagement in a time of testing pressures is particularly challenging. Inevitably, a dilemma in a democratic school is teaching about democracy versus modeling democratic decisionmaking processes. In the chapters ahead, we see examples of teacher choice to participate and examples, as well as other initiatives, that required the participation of all.

This section provides cases of how schools can be open for variability of implementation, while at the same time adhering to clear and consistent goals. Principal Shannon created opportunities in which teachers could try out the idea of fostering civic engagement on their own terms. She balanced this "opt-in" approach with creating activities and structures that demanded participation. These activities required spaces to serve as a way to define the culture of the school as "the way we do things here," including the value of student participation.

Leadership may not expect all teachers to be on board, but it must provide opportunities to safely "try out" civic engagement and expand possibilities for such opportunities to occur. An upper-grade teacher reflected on Principal Shannon's leadership style:

Shannon has phenomenal ideas, and I think that she knows where she wants us to be. But I'm not sure that the process to get us there is fully democratic. And that's hard. . . . I have no problem with these great ideas being floated from all points, but I think that initiatives in a "democratic" atmosphere need to be "of the people, for the people, by the people," otherwise we are not operating under democratic principles. . . . I feel that [democracy at Dewey is] at a fledgling state. I think that it ebbs and flows. I think it gains momentum . . . but it's two steps forward, one step back. I think that's how democracy works. We're a microcosm of the greater democracy that we exist in. . . . Shannon is in a really strange position of being in a public school, accountable to the public and a school board, and NCLB. She is . . . serving two masters because she can't relinquish 100% control, because she has other people that she has to answer to. . . . She's in a really difficult position to be a truly democratic leader.

Despite the need to keep the vision of the school clear, the chapters in this section demonstrate the tension between democratic processes and maintaining a consistent vision for civic change. The chapters suggest that *how* decisions occur matters—often even more than *what* occurs. They raise the question of whether a mandated vision is needed to preserve civic ideals in a time of accountability pressures.

Overall, these chapters consider schoolwide structures and processes that keep civic engagement alive. Through these explorations, we look at lessons from Dewey for leaders who seek to maintain a civic vision for their schools. We consider the importance of balancing a strong school vision while allowing for a collaborative decisionmaking process. We also consider the agency teachers have to participate and initiate civic engagement activities.

Looking ahead, Chapter 5 describes a schoolwide environmental initiative. Schoolyard provided teachers with significant release time to plan intentionally how to incorporate environmental concepts into their classrooms. Chapter 6 discusses All-School Assemblies (ASAs), which created a weekly gathering space for the entire school. Although many schools have an assembly period, the ASA differs in that it was designed with a clear civic vision. Weekly values were introduced, and students who exemplified these values were celebrated. Classes shared the ongoing work that they were doing on civic engagement activities. Chapter 7 discusses Small School Advisories, which served as a setting for cross-age groups of children from kindergarten to the 5th grade to meet monthly with a teacher in the school. Students keep the same advisory throughout their time at Dewey. This structure provided a way for children to be known better in the school community and created another structure for developing service learning and other civic-minded activities.

CHAPTER 5

Environmental Stewardship
Giving Teachers Reasons to Participate

As students begin to trickle into the classroom, Mr. Clark greets them and prepares the room and the day's activities. He rearranges the tables and chairs so that the students can sit in a circle or semicircle. Students coming in help set up the room while they talk with one another and explore the classroom.

After the chairs are set up, Mr. Clark asks, "What kind of living things are living around us?" This sparks a conversation about the environment immediately surrounding Dewey Elementary. Amanda, a 3rd-grader, answers, "There are tadpoles. I remember from last year—they're living in the wetlands."

Mr. Clark then tells the students to leave all their materials at their desks and to line up to go outside. They head out on a "nature walk" of the school grounds. As they gather in the woods on Dewey's property, Mr. Clark talks to the students about the trees that surround them and what kind of animals might live in those trees. The students stop mid-stride as a squirrel scurries past them. One student points out a large nest above their heads. Mr. Clark asks what animals live in nests and what nests are made of and gives a long answer about "hard and soft mast" in forests.

As the students move deeper into the woods, a 3rd-grade student, Justin, notices a hornet's nest on the ground. He is excited to have found a nest because the group has just discussed flying insects living at Dewey.

Mr. Clark points out the wetlands and wooded areas of the school grounds. A student asks about the "biggest plants they can think of," which the class decides are trees. As they continue the discussion, Mr. Clark walks them over to a cross-section of a tree trunk. The kids huddle tightly around the trunk. Mr. Clark talks about what you can learn from the rings. One of the students counts the number of rings and announces the age of the tree.

To move the discussion along, Mr. Clark asks, "Are trees just a big pole?" Several students respond by saying that they have branches. Taking a cue from this, Mr. Clark takes out a pile of "tree cookies"—smaller cross-sections of tree branches. He presents the "cookies," which had holes drilled in them already, to the students, and announces that they will be making the tree cookies into nametags to wear as a group.

As the students finished making their nametags, they bring the cookies to Mr. Clark, who strings them for the students to wear as a necklace nametag. Near the end of their meeting, Mr. Clark turns the conversation to how they could save trees and use them wisely. A 3rd-grader, Amanda, offers the idea that they should all recycle.

Mr. Clark agrees and asks rhetorically, "Would we like to plant more trees?" (Mr. Clark had already planned that the students would plant trees.) Although the students do not have much reaction to the question, Mr. Clark continues: "Next time, we'll go for a walk around Dewey and see if there are places where we need more trees." He announces that the following weeks will be organized around the plan to plant trees around the school.

Although Dewey is located in a small college town, its wooded campus is not unusual in size or scope for an elementary school. What is unusual is how teachers and Principal Shannon make use of all the grounds as an expanded teaching and learning space. Dewey's students explore the world outside of the classroom walls as much as inside. Seeking out partnerships with community organizations and state officials has transformed Dewey's grounds into an outdoor learning laboratory. The grounds of the school include a wetland, a garden, a nature trail, an outdoor amphitheater, a butterfly garden, and a teepee. According to a report written by Principal Shannon and a graduate student from the local university, Brenda Black:

> Two Eagle Scout projects have been completed, including nature trail refurbishment and an animal observation area. Another Eagle Scout project is in the early stages of planning an amphitheater. A local nursery donated the services of a landscape architect to design a butterfly garden that 5th-graders have integrated into their math instruction. The area has become a data collection research area for the national project Monarch Watch. It is also an area of community service with local Girl Scouts, Brownies, and the Dewey Parent Teacher Organization (PTO) assisting and maintaining the garden during the summer months. Master Gardeners have been involved in numerous gardening projects at Dewey. Adjacent to the butterfly garden is a composting area where Dewey composts lunchtime waste as part of an Earth Force Project for 5th-graders. The school site offers numerous picnic areas that are used by community members in the evening and over the summer. Another Earth Force Project in the planning stages is to plant a nursery of trees. Each kindergartner will be given a tree so that the child and his/her parent(s) can see the analogous relationship between the tree's growth and the child's growth over the school years.

These environmental projects emerge out of an intersection of the other pieces of the school's mission—a focus on inquiry, student voice, environment, and partnering with the community. They highlight spaces for place-based learning and help young people think of ways to study and care for their communities. Kindergarten teacher Mrs. Smith observed: "Well, I really do admire some of the things Principal Shannon has done in terms of the nature journals and bettering our school environment. Going green in a way. She empowers the kids, and I would have to say I do that as well."

PLACE-BASED LEARNING INSPIRES TEACHER COLLABORATION

A focal point for environmental work at Dewey was Schoolyard—a 5-year professional development initiative to use the outdoor space of the school grounds as a laboratory for teaching and learning about place-based education and the environment. This project built on Dewey's civic goals to provide ways to create authentic learning environments for students in which they could ask meaningful questions, conduct inquiries on real-world problems, and reflect on the agency that they might have to explore their world. These processes further helped young people consider the impact of their lives on the environment and explore ways to make a difference as a process of environmental stewardship.

To design and implement the Schoolyard project, Dewey received grants from the state's Department of Environmental Protection and Department of Education. Principal Shannon prepared the grant proposals written in collaboration with Dewey teachers and graduate student Brenda Black. Shannon and Black explained Schoolyard as a "data collection, research-based, schoolwide community building initiative involving the phenology of the PFE school site." Participating classes engaged in activities once a month in which they gathered data from the environment, including temperature, rainfall, and bird migration. Shannon and Black designed the program in conjunction with the construction of a new school building for Dewey. They explained in their grant proposal:

> [We will] have children look at the new school site, which was dramatically altered by demolition of the former building and the construction of a new one, and offer ideas as to how to use the new site. [Classrooms will explore] four outdoor areas once a month. [Students will keep] observation journals and submit data/observation sheets describing the observations of the four areas, including the rainfall and temperature. Those data/observation sheets [will be placed] in a schoolwide journal for each site. The four schoolwide journals provide a record of daily observations, and the data records about our school site's change over time (the phenology).

The activities in the Schoolyard project often developed from student-initiated projects about their environment. Student voice drove learning goals. Principal Shannon invited teachers to participate in Schoolyard. She explained:

> We talked about what our goals and hopes were and said, "If you want to be a part of this, [that's] fine! It's purely voluntary. We'd like you to develop an action plan, do monthly reflections. We'll give you a half-day release time. We'll have midyear and end-of-year celebrations to recognize everyone's good work." The numbers for the program increased gradually, until now all but one teacher in the school has participated actively in the project.

Teachers resoundingly spoke of Schoolyard as an exciting option—from the teachers who are always ready for a new project to the reluctant teachers who do not always agree with Shannon's ideas. Providing release time and praising success in the program were strategic ways for Shannon to grow civic engagement practices. She explained:

> It's purely voluntary . . . and I've not pestered them about "why," or "You sure you don't want to consider?" This has to evolve organically, so we will just let it go. All 12 interns [student teachers also] are involved this year. So, not only are the interns learning from the teachers, but the teachers are learning from them. They are collaborating together, and nobody's dictating what they do. They plan their own agendas.

The few who did not participate originally did so for important personal reasons, including facing extensive familial pressures that year and taking on other important school and district leadership roles. Eventually all but one teacher took part in Schoolyard.

At the heart of the Schoolyard vision was the power of teacher collaboration as a way to deepen high-quality practice. Fifth-grade teacher Ms. Uday commented: "The Schoolyard project has enabled [teacher] teams to start seeing the power and the benefit of collaboration." The interest in participating is then reinforced through collaboration as well. Shannon encouraged teachers to work in teams on the Schoolyard project. Uday explained:

> I think the teachers do a lot collaborating together. I think what we've done with Schoolyard has really brought them around to moving from having a learning community to a community of practice . . . they work together to solve things. What it has done in the culture in the school is that they are looking to one another to solve problems and to build their community in that way. Well, they are helping each other make this work. They are sharing with each other. That culture of sharing has been here somewhat but it has been limited to teams. It's now crossing those boundaries of teams. Not just with whom you work. It's with everybody. And that's what you want. "Okay, I have this problem, can I get a group of people together to think about it?" Rather than, "Here's my problem and I dump it on the principal." It becomes the practice of what they do.

Teams of teachers received paid release time to plan their projects. Teachers each received a booklet that included the purpose of the Schoolyard project, connections to state standards, and some ideas for how to get started. "This guide provided support while maintaining teacher autonomy," according to the report written by Black and Shannon to the granting agency. Teachers used half and full days off from teaching to meet in one another's houses to think about how to revise their practice to incorporate innovative methods and ideas. They reviewed student artifacts—journals, data sheets, and projects—to reflect on their work and to plan for the next steps. Second-grade teacher Ms. Jones was an expert in reading intervention. She tended to view many Dewey initiatives as taking away from teaching and learning. In this project, rather, she embraced Schoolyard as a way to deepen her practice in ways that she valued:

> I've been on [Schoolyard] for 3 years. The first 2 years, it was mostly all the teachers in the primary division . . . it was a study group. We studied how to best implement Schoolyard with our students. We shared lesson plans . . . and we usually would test them and in the meetings we would share how they went.
>
> This year I'm on a different group. It's myself and a couple of primary teachers, and a lot of the interns. This year we're trying to see if we can better integrate our measurement unit in math in Schoolyard. . . . Measurement is typically the last unit we teach. A lot of things are happening at the end of the school year, and it sometimes gets cheated and short-changed. We wanted to see if we could integrate it more naturally being taught all throughout the year instead of depending on the last 6 weeks that it needs to be taught. . . . I really love the way the meeting times are set up because it's much more teacher-directed, again. Teachers have the freedom to decide what we're going to study as a group; we set the meeting times, we set the meeting place, we make our own agendas.

All of the teachers in our observations and interviews raved about the level of professionalism associated with the Schoolyard project, including the ability to leave school grounds and to reflect without heavy-handed monitoring by Shannon. Kindergarten teacher Ms. Smith, another teacher whose expertise and interests did not always align with Principal Shannon's vision, explained: "Schoolyard is an opt-in for me. I need to have that extra push to get in the nature stuff. I am able to plan my own activity. We get to plan together. We get the respect that we are going to work when we are supposed to."

The planning time provided an organizational support that created "a safe space for reflection and refinement," according to Black and Shannon's proposal. Other teachers met monthly to engage in book study groups. This range of self-directed projects helped teachers "engage as professional learners, refine themselves as a community of learners, and develop cross-divisional relationships," according to a follow-up report to the grant-making agency written by Black and Shannon.

CONNECTING SCHOOLYARD TO THE CIVIC VISION

Buy-in allowed for teachers to get their feet wet in something new without administrative pressure. The opt-in environment allowed other teachers to flourish in trying out new civic practices without administrative constraints on their own professional development. Two 5th-grade teachers, Ms. Owen and Ms. Uday, seized on the Schoolyard project as a way to extend their literacy curriculum. In response to their dissatisfaction to the 5th-grade writing curriculum, made up of traditional "writing prompts," they met with Shannon and asked permission to re-vamp their own writing curriculum because they noticed how motivated their students were to make their own choices about what to write about their Schoolyard. Shannon encouraged them to try out their idea. They worked with each of their students to follow a line of inquiry, chosen by the individual student, from the Schoolyard experience. One student wanted to know if all compost was equal and if certain types of plants grew better in various compost varieties. Students worked to collect data but also put their inquiry and findings into a kid-friendly zine on their scientific inquiry. The 5th-grade teachers later adapted the zine project's subject area focus to be civic (as described in chapter 4, the civic zines). In addition to the pupils' inquiries, the two 5th-grade teachers collected data on student engagement (time spent on task, reported enjoyment) and district-level writing scores to find out if this method was really more meaningful to students than their previous writing curriculum.

A 3rd-grade teacher, Mr. Tyler, aligned Schoolyard with a broader service-learning activity for his class:

> We terra-cycle the milk bottle caps because bottle caps are usually not recyclable. Another teacher handles the actual bottles himself, and we do the caps. We also do terra-cycling with four other things: Ziploc bags, plastic tape dispensers, Elmer glue sticks, and Capri Sun pouches or any juice pouch. And the terra-cycling is . . . have you ever seen anything like a purse made out of Capri Sun pouches? They make clipboards out of the Ziploc. Usually Ziploc bags and things like that are nonrecyclable, so you can't do anything with them and they end up going in the dump. So we collect those things, ship them off to the company; they make products out of them. They pay us per pound. But it's not really for the money.

Ms. Jones, the 2nd-grade reading expert, expanded on her use of the environmental concerns with a student-initiated research process that could link principles of scientific questioning, student voice, inquiry, service-learning, and environmental stewardship. This vignette provides an example of a Schoolyard activity that she conducted in her classroom:

Students gather on the rug of Ms. Jones's room to continue their work on their social studies unit called Going Green. Ms. Jones asks the children to think about how composting already occurs at Dewey. The children discuss the elaborate bins in the lunchroom designed to minimize food waste, and talk about why composting helps the environment and what happens in the compost bin to break down the food into soil.

"What if we eat an apple as a snack in our classroom?" a student asks.

"You should compost that apple core!" another responds.

"Well, we don't really have any way to do that in our classroom to collect it," responds Ms. Jones.

"You could just take it to the compost bin in the teacher's lounge where they have lunch!" a student suggests.

Ms. Jones hesitates, and then explains, "We don't compost in the teacher's lounge."

The students erupt with outbursts of concern.

"Why not?"

"No way!"

"What do you mean the teachers don't compost?"

"What can we do about this?"

Ms. Jones reflected later, "To me that's what I wanted to have happen. It was one of those teachable moments. Jones was teaching a writing unit at the same time called Writing for Change. She explained:

> It all just kind of came together. I look for opportunities like that rather than just sort of trying to go, "Hey, we should do this." They don't really have any buy-in to it. It was exciting to see that happen. They wrote letters to the faculty [about the need for teacher's lounge composting]. They wrote letters to the 5th-grade class to ask for help. They had written letters to the principal to ask, "Can we buy some things to help us do this?" It turned into that, and that was exciting to see.

Jones looked for "aha moments" emerging from the students themselves as a way to combine environmental stewardship, service learning, student voice, and inquiry. She explained, "I've been struggling with trying to find—I don't want to do something like, 'Oh, let's put a jar in people's rooms and collect money for something.' A lot of that happens, and I'm not sure it's meaningful for the kids. I'm looking for those things that come out of the students themselves."

Looking at the outcomes of the Schoolyard project overall, surveys of students conducted by Principal Shannon and Black indicated that students valued the opportunities for place-based learning. Teachers, for their part, reported appreciating opportunities for action research and sought ways to deepen their experiences by integrating Schoolyard activities with district curricula in future lessons. These opportunities to teach environmental stewardship helped model ways in which the school was connected to the broader community and showed little and large ways that students could make a difference in the world.

LESSONS FOR PRACTICE

Broaden conceptions of civic engagement beyond political participation. Although traditional notions of civic engagement focus on active participation in political processes, Dewey's experiences highlight the growing connection occurring in many venues between participation in public life. The definition of public life and civil society extends beyond people to include the globe itself—the trees, the oceans, the planet. Zukin, Keeter, Andolina, Jenkins, and Carpini (2006) have shown that young people are "quite active" in a "more private, civic sphere of activity" (p. viii)—a sphere that includes volunteering, being active in one's own local community, and making consumer or lifestyle choices based on political considerations. Other studies likewise have emphasized how young people are more inclined toward more personal and community-based civic activities than traditional forms of politics, like voting (Flanagan, 2013; Sherrod, Torney-Purta, & Flanagan, 2010; Westheimer & Kahne, 2004). Younger generations especially value a closer tie between environmental stewardship and civil society (Harris, Wyn, & Younes, 2010). Curricular and learning opportunities in schools should reflect this shift in civic values.

Turn the school and environment into a living laboratory for practicing civic action. When the school facilities and surrounding areas are defined as spaces where young people can take action, they serve as a broadened public arena for young learners to understand how to design a change effort and take action. Encouraging students to be careful observers of their lives and scaffolding opportunities to question why things occur and how to make changes empowers young people to see concrete ways in which they can make a difference. Such processes can also expand student opinions to consider how changes would impact the entire school community and not just themselves.

Increase teacher buy-in and deepen outcomes with opt-in strategies for reform. Although the Schoolyard effort is purely voluntary, almost all teachers in the school chose to participate. Because they were able to choose to opt in to a change effort, teachers were more willing to dive into the effort rather than resist what was forced upon them. This structuring of change helped foster enthusiasm for the effort and sparked creativity rather than resistance.

Build a positive climate and improve teaching and learning by encouraging teacher professionalism. The Schoolyard model recognized teachers as experts, as leaders, and as contributors to a reform initiative—all roles shown to enhance the positive outcomes of professional development (Belzer, 2005). As Black and Shannon explained in their grant report, "the original intent was to foster teacher autonomy, creativity, and subject integration by having minimal guidelines when taking students outdoors." Flexibility increases relevance for teachers. Research indicates that relevance, practicality, and application are central to professional development opportunities; they are more likely to influence the taught curriculum (Fogarty & Pete, 2007; Glickman, Gordon, & Ross-Gordon, 2004). This expectation that teachers will bring enthusiasm, talent, and their own ways of enacting curricular goals can deepen implementation of a reform and help ensure the sustainability of the effort (Coburn, 2003) because teachers have greater ownership of the content and process.

Value collaboration. The Schoolyard design included the assumption that collaboration could improve the development of the project. Creating time and space for collaboration, and reducing constraints on what the collaboration looked like, not only deepened the content of Schoolyard, but it also inspired the spread of Schoolyard principles into other parts of the school day, as we saw when Ms. Jones engaged her class in the compost inquiry project and a 5th-grade science zine project.

The process of collaboration also helped reinforce the value of a community of learners at Dewey, encouraging teachers to value one another as resources and support mechanisms. As we have described previously (Brezicha, Bergmark, & Mitra, 2015), educational leaders have a responsibility to help structure the social environment to encourage a professional community of teachers (Coburn & Stein, 2006; Leithwood & Poplin, 1992). Teachers can strengthen civic engagement practices through interaction with others in formal and informal processes. Teacher collaboration can encourage positive feedback and support that could help the reform idea become a self-sustaining initiative (Blase & Blase, 2000). By exchanging ideas and interpretations of policies, teachers construct shared understandings and adjust their own professional stance on their teaching goals and practice (Coburn, 2006).

Funding signals that an idea has value. Furthermore, small monies that allow time for teacher collaboration can pay off as big dividends for changing practice. The small grants at Dewey provided the gift of time. Even the smallest pots of money can give time for teachers to collaborate, which can in turn lead to deep and meaningful new ideas.

CHAPTER 6

All-School Assemblies
Creating a Schoolwide Vision for Civic Engagement

Supporting civic learning in elementary schools includes developing consistent structures that establish and eventually reify visions of civic engagement. This chapter highlights the value of creating school structures that protect and emphasize the value of students, teachers, and staff across a school gathering together regularly as a community. All-School Assemblies (ASAs) created a sense of school community at Dewey. The ritual of coming together, singing songs, and celebrating successes served as a way to create a common vision at the school that emphasized the values of democracy, community, student voice, and environment. Celebrations, such as on Dr. Seuss's birthday, for Earth Day, and for teacher milestones, helped build community. Through singing and rituals in a regular weekly format, the ASAs anchored the community at Dewey. Music sets a joyous mood; either the music teacher or a student plays the piano or other instrument as the student body enters and exits, and almost every week there is a musical accompaniment—often by a teacher but sometimes by students as well.

Students file into the school's all-purpose room—a space that serves as the gymnasium, cafeteria, and auditorium. Rather than using the stage at the end of the room, the focal point of the gathering is the center of the room, allowing all students to feel closer to the activities. Students sit on the floor in a U-shape, and the teachers sit on chairs in a U-shaped row behind them. The student leaders for that week's assembly are situated in the front of the middle of the U, with a microphone and a makeshift podium, most often a music stand.

A teacher and student begin to play "The Farmer in the Dell" on the piano as classes take a seat on the floor. The principal begins to clap along with the music, and many students join in. Everyone is noisy as they enter the room. Teachers are standing around chatting while students continue to arrive.

The 5th-graders have a table set up in the middle for the projector, which projects on the wall behind the piano player. They are looking over a paper together. The piano is still going strong, now playing "When the Saints Go Marching In." Two teachers start dancing together, and many students clap along with the music. Two 5th-grade girls (the leaders for today) raise their hands to silence everyone, and the crowd quickly quiets down.

One of the 5th-grade announcers steps forward to the microphone and says, "We will begin with a presentation on energy saving."

She hands the microphone to 3 students. "Hi, Dewey Elementary School!" They then introduce themselves by their first names. They give some background on their project from last year. "In science, we had a unit on energy. Mrs. Martin walked us around the building for an energy audit. We wanted to see if we could find wasted energy.

"After that, we met with Mr. Marks (he is in charge of all the buildings in our district). We told him that we noticed the small round lights outside our doors and we thought they were a good representation of a lot of wasted energy. Mr. Marks came to our school and we shared the idea to turn off those lights and see if it made much of a difference [in energy savings]. Whenever we just turn off the lights it will save so much energy! We can even turn off laptops when we are not using them. We can turn them off and save money and save a lot and the money can go to supplies in your classroom. So you see, Dewey, everything we do can make such a big difference. Turn off the faucet! Turn off the lights when it is sunny!"

The three students say in unison, "We need your help, Dewey Elementary School!" Everyone applauds.

ASAs provided the 5th-graders (the school's most senior students) with leadership opportunities. Beyond the weekly rituals, the 5th-graders have a degree of free time that they can fill with whatever kind of activity they wish. Examples of what the students have done with this time include, but are not limited to, guessing games, sharing artwork, readings from favorite poets, songs, skits and discussions of current events, encouragement for standardized tests, and "kudos"— expressions of appreciation to fellow students and teachers.

Leading ASAs served as a hallmark of student voice and leadership for the oldest students at Dewey. The student leadership of ASAs has come to be viewed as a rite of passage for the 5th-graders in the school. One teacher verbalized that the younger kids are beginning to "aspire to be . . . or look forward to this great experience of leading All-School."

The ASA is accomplished with a minimum of teacher involvement. Teachers mostly help with logistical and technological issues. The students use a shared Google Doc to collaborate on ASA planning and share their work with their teachers and Principal Shannon before the weekly gathering. Student leadership is authentic in this activity; teachers defer to student ideas, cues, and directions. In fact, the teachers tend to act like "students"; they chat with one another or sing and clap along with the music just like the rest of the students until the 5th-graders take the floor and call the assembly to attention, typically by saying, "If you can hear my voice clap once, clap twice," or even just by raising a silent hand in the air, which usually works to bring the room to order.

For the past 2 years, the final ASA of the school year has included the whole school lining the hallways to applaud the graduating 5th-graders. In the words of a primary-grade teacher:

> We embraced the 5th-graders as they were leaving. They came down the stairs and went through our hallways. We all came out of the rooms and cheered and clapped for them, because we knew that was it; they're going to middle school. . . . There's a lot of good coming out of that, and it's evolving as well.

The primary-grade teacher then recounted how as their photos flashed on a slide-show screen, almost all of the students said aloud the name of every graduating 5th-grader. This activity has helped encourage Dewey 5th-graders to remember the school as a supportive, caring community.

VALUING ENVIRONMENTAL STEWARDSHIP AND SERVICE-LEARNING PROJECTS

In an ASA later that year, Mrs. Green's 3rd-grade class presents about their efforts to raise money to help with the Gulf oil spill. Three girls—Olivia, Natalie, and Emily report that they received a letter from the National Audubon Society thanking them for the $358 that they sent in. The girls thank everyone for their help and there is a big cheer.

The lead 5th-graders then call up 2nd-grade teacher Mr. Tyler with a group of his students. Mr. Tyler reminds everyone that his class is still collecting bottle caps to be recycled this year. One of his students explains about the recycling of the breakfast milk bottles. This class thought of the idea that although the lunch milk bottles were recycled, the breakfast ones were not. So, we placed recycling buckets in each classroom to avoid milk bottles being placed in the trash.

The students in this class then focus on trash cleanup. The first one says, "There is trash on the school playground and elsewhere."

Another students exclaims, "Encourage your classmates to pick up trash!"'

A third student says, "Shout out 'Go green' if you think you can make a difference!"

All the students in the audience shout, "Go green!"

At the end of the presenting all of the students say in unison, "We need your help, Dewey Elementary School!"

ASAs served as a platform for students to present projects to the student body—often related to civic action goals of service learning and environmental stewardship. Examples included a group of 5th-grade girls working with school and district lunch officials to add a no-meat, no-dairy salad to the districtwide lunch menu (discussed in the next section), and 1st-graders engaging in a campaign to reduce paper towel wastage, thereby significantly reducing both financial and environmental waste. The weekly ASA also served as a forum for celebrating and validating various civic action projects that result from a teacher or student-driven inquiry within classrooms. Projects included schoolwide composting, sending books to Africa, developing a relationship with the local homeless shelter, and building a wetland on the school property.

The 5th-grade announcers call up 1st/2nd combined class teacher Mr. Hoffsteader. Along with his students, Mr. Hoffsteader shares their success with the state paper-recycling competition. The 1st- and 2nd-grade students take turns reporting on how much paper they use at Dewey.
  One student says, "684 pounds of paper is the same as this many sheets of paper." Another explains, "Last year we came in seventh place in the competition." A third adds, "The contest is from October 1 to 31."
  Then the rest of the class carries in empty boxes to show how many boxes of paper they recycled last year during the contest, so that everyone would be able to visualize the amount. More than 20 empty paper boxes are stacked in front of the students.
  Mr. Hoffsteader reminds everyone that it had been only 1 month of recycling, and look how much paper they used! He says, "We use a lot of paper at Dewey Elementary. Hey, thumbs up if you think you can recycle next month even more than usual."
  All the students in the audience put their thumbs up.

Presentations at ASAs often had a civic theme and end with a call to action such as "We also want you to know that by working together you can make a difference at Dewey Elementary." On another occasion, after discussing Earth Day (a day in April in which environmental activities occur in the United States) and the need to keep their school trash-free, the 5th-graders gave an award to the janitor for being the best janitor.

TEACHING CITIZENSHIP GOALS

The ASAs reinforced civics messages through weekly rituals, including the "value of the week" focus that is common in many elementary schools. Each week, the 5th-graders prepared a skit to highlight the citizenship theme of the week, such as honesty and compassion. Children received citizenship rewards for reflecting this character trait. Classrooms also received "Penguin (school mascot) Awards" for exemplifying character traits.

It was time for the weekly presentation of stuffed animal Penguins (the school mascot) to students who had most exhibited the character trait of the week in each classroom that week. "The trait this week is honesty," said the 5th-grade announcer. "We would like the following students to come forward to receive the Penguin awards for their ability to speak truth in a kind and generous manner." Students from each grade level were announced, and handed the stuffed penguins that rotated among classrooms weekly. The students stood in a line with beaming faces. Afterward, a song signaled that the ASA had come to an end for the week, and students filed out and went back to their classes.

BUILDING A SHARED VISION THROUGH MANDATORY ACTIVITIES

The structure of ASAs exemplifies a school policy initiated by Principal Shannon that became a part of the culture of Dewey Elementary. The idea behind ASAs, in Shannon's words, is that they are a venue for civic engagement that is "student-to-student." Shannon established nonnegotiable components of fostering civic engagement, such as all classes attending ASA. Over time, ASAs have become the "way we do things here." She trusted that most teachers will eventually "get it," whereas a minority will never buy into a social or civic mission for schools, as is the case for most change efforts that occur in schools.

Despite the success of ASAs, many teachers in the school were initially resistant to the idea. ASAs highlight how process can detract from a promising school climate when democratic decisionmaking does not occur or decisionmaking is not perceived to have been "democratic enough." An upper-grade teacher explained:

> Shannon gets an idea in her mind and she focuses on it, and she goes for it. Sometimes that's to the detriment of the cohesiveness of our staff. Because then it kind of divides us sometimes, because there are those of us who are there and will do the best we can with what we have. And some who are, "No, I'm good with what I had going on. Why do you need to throw another iron in the fire?"

This teacher's perspective highlights the need at times to assert a vision even when all teachers are not on board—but such strategies can only happen so many times or teachers will become overwhelmed. Indeed, in our last 2 years of data collection at Dewey, Principal Shannon did not implement any new initiatives. She told us this was because "So much is going on. Teachers need time to incorporate all that we have begun in recent years. They are telling me they don't want anything else that is new right now." Sustaining civic initiatives is only possible if at some point practices become embedded in the day-to-day functioning of the school.

Conflict among school staff can be challenging—and especially in elementary school contexts that tend to be conflict-adverse settings. Even with concerns about the ASA, no confrontation occurred about the new program. Our survey of Dewey teachers indicates resistance about focusing on civic activities from a small group of Dewey teachers (~15%). At the other end of the spectrum, in a survey that we conducted, about 25% of Dewey teachers strongly supported

Shannon's leadership style. Based on these figures, it is clear that most teachers just kind of go with the flow.

One primary teacher explained the tension between having concerns but norms in the practice of not speaking up.

> Staff meetings are wonderful. All of us together talking about what is going on. [But] there seems to be just this ... [feeling of] ... "I don't want to speak up." In a school where we're *trying* to be open and have discourse ... I think a lot of us are [conflict-averse]. I think that's what draws a lot of us to elementary school. . . . It's a democracy aspect. But I think in a true function of a democracy, people have to be able to speak their mind. [There is no] dictatorship here. People are [not] afraid to speak their mind because of consequences. I think it's that people are afraid to have conflict.

The concerns that persisted about ASA ended up being concentrated primarily among teachers in the lower grades. For these classes, students were less likely to participate in the ASAs and also less able to sit "watching" through the entire presentation. The younger students were expected to learn how to sit attentively. Students who could not sit quietly were occasionally removed from the room by Shannon and teachers. A kindergarten teacher commented:

> In the beginning, it was a pain [to take our children to ASA]. We meet once a week, teach once a month. That was our initial feeling. But I had a son in that original cohort [of 5th-grade presenters]. . . . Since [then] I have gained an appreciation of the event. I saw the impact it had on my son. It is valuable to them [the 5th-grade students]. A big school decision that was made and now has taken hold. With any decision you have to try it out. Forty minutes is a long time for kindergarten, but the benefits outweigh the drawbacks.

As ASAs evolved, more teachers indicated more support. Shannon reported that a specialist teacher who was especially skeptical of the ASA meetings came to her this year and said, "I get it now," as she saw the ways in which the community came together around ASAs. There is also the belief that as ASA has become more established, to be a 5th-grader and have the opportunity to lead an ASA is something to which the younger students look forward. As one teacher explained, "So I think it's going to be that they're going to aspire to be ... or look forward to this great experience of leading All-School. But it's new for them."

LESSONS FOR PRACTICE

The structure of the All-School Assembly offered a communal space for valuing the work of civic engagement. The processes and rituals associated with ASAs align well with previous research on authentic participation (Lundy,

2007)—space, voice, audience, and influence are supports that make All-School Assemblies a powerful space for celebrating civic action.

Develop consistent structures to provide sustainability for a civic engagement vision. Looking at the structures in place at Dewey Elementary, we saw the ways in which the ASA served as a consistent space for celebrating, amplifying, and valuing civic engagement. The regularity of these structures built into the school calendar meant that extra energy was not needed to build spaces for civic engagement. Rather, the structure created a vessel that begged to be filled by civic activities. Even as standardized testing pressures increased and some teachers wished for more instructional time to devote to reading and math, Principal Shannon protected this space as valued and central to the school's mission. Strong leadership in democratic schools can help create, maintain, and support spaces for the processes of civic engagement.

Create spaces for celebration. ASAs provided a public space, the democratic polis for Dewey that provides an opportunity for celebration. They were a space for articulating shared values of civic engagement and for acknowledging the civic actions occurring in the school. The assemblies were overwhelmingly upbeat. They provided a space for enthusiasm, recognition of talents, and often laughter. Singing and clapping of hands was the norm at the end and beginning of the assemblies. On a basic level, ASAs provided an opportunity to include opportunities for laughter and building community in the school day. Through such optimistic experiences, they helped foster a positive school climate.

Have students take the lead. Student-led schoolwide assemblies highlight the value of students as members of the school community. Such activities amplify student voice. Students feel that their voices matter and feel heard. Increased student voice has been shown to improve school reform outcomes (Fielding, 2001; Mitra, 2008), increase the belief that young people can make a difference, and build the assets that young people need to be successful (Camino & Zeldin, 2002; Mitra & Serriere, 2012). At Dewey, the 5th-graders ran the show at ASAs, although students of all ages participated in specific presentations and activities. The 5th-graders were pushed to take on leadership roles and gained a sense of visibility for the school climate in the process. The final celebration at the end of the year, celebrating their graduation from Dewey, modeled the valuing of students and their roles in the school community.

Build a positive climate through shared celebration to build trust among students and teachers. ASAs were a space for the celebration of successes. They served as places for articulating shared values of civic engagement and for acknowledging students' work. ASAs created a space for emphasizing belonging to the school—an important building block for healthy and academically successful kids (Mitra, 2004; Mitra & Serriere, 2012; Roeser, Midgley, & Urdan, 1996).

Identify and share visible victories. ASAs provided a structured audience for recognizing civic action. Such an audience can validate civic work by offering a space for visible victories, which helps validate inquiry and civic engagement. Our previous work has shown the importance of sharing civic engagement work so that students can feel that their work is valued. Visible victories (McLaughlin, 1993) such as the presentations at ASA can boost morale and establish the credibility of a change effort. They can illustrate the significance of civic engagement to young people (Denner, Meyer, & Bean, 2005; Mitra, 2004, 2009a). A space for visible victories both emphasizes the value of civic engagement work and gives energy and renewed enthusiasm for continuing it. Creating an audience for civic engagement provides a space for young people to frame their civic work and present it to an audience.

The public nature of the ASA presentations also make them useful tools for sharing the work of the school and individual teacher practice at other professional venues. Teachers use videos from All-School Assemblies to share the work of the school during professional development sessions, conference presentations, district meetings, and individual portfolio development. For example, two Dewey teacher interns developed a video for their teaching portfolio that showed how the 1st- and 2nd-grade students reduced paper towel wastage by making signs to place on all of the school's towel dispensers. The video filmed the students presenting this work during an ASA. In this presentation, the students demonstrated, with physical data, the difference between how many boxes of paper towels are used in the school when students used one paper towel to dry their hands versus three towels. After that presentation, paper towel waste dropped dramatically schoolwide and the students shared their message with other schools in the district. This project was notable for its blending of service learning and inquiry with a reinforcement of schoolwide values, such as environmentalism, through All-School Assemblies. The video also provided a visual and interactive way for the teachers to explain their practice in other professional venues.

CHAPTER 7

Small School Advisories
Making Implementation Variable

As a complement to weekly All-School Assemblies, children at Dewey meet regularly with a small group of students and an adult, called Small School Advisories (SSAs)—an alternative social, civic, and academic small group. SSAs were introduced a few years after the ASAs to ensure that all children would develop a caring, stable relationship with an adult in the school and to build community between grades. Influenced by her friendships in the League of Democratic Schools founded by John Goodlad, Principal Shannon sought to implement a cross-age advisory system in the school.

All children at Dewey Elementary have monthly SSA time. In every SSA, approximately 12–14 kindergartners to 5th-graders meet once a month for 40 minutes (eight times a year) with their assigned teacher. Students remained with their SSA teacher throughout their 6 years at Dewey Elementary. Principal Shannon emphasized the value of SSAs serving as "a platform for people to become active in the school." She hoped that SSAs would spur teachers to "begin to look at other ways to make our school a better place, to find ways to improve whatever the problem is that they come up with."

CREATE TEAMS OF TEACHERS TO
IMPLEMENT NEW IDEAS

To bring the idea of SSAs into practice, Principal Shannon convened a working group over the summer of six teachers with a range of teaching experiences as well as a range of support for the idea. The convening group decided to quickly implement the SSA plan—the small-group advisories began schoolwide that September.

The plan for SSAs was introduced to teachers as they returned to school for the new school year. Teacher Howard led the presentation. As one of the most senior teachers in the school and a strong supporter of the concept, she participated in the summer planning and led the presentation to faculty. Standing at the front of the school's all-purpose room as teachers sat at circular cafeteria tables. Ms. Howard couched the initiative in the language of community building and caring relationships. She told her colleagues:

Our expertise is connecting with kids and making a difference with the kids and for the kids. This is what excites us, connecting with kids. . . . In all of our classes, we can identify children who are quiet but have something to say, whom we'd like to get to know better.

Howard then shared the five purposes developed by the planning committee: "To connect children with an adult for all 6 years at the school (K–5); build a small, supportive community structure; provide a forum for discussion about all school topics; reach consensus about items relevant to the whole school; and identify issues and topics of importance to everyone."

Participation in SSAs was mandatory for all the school's teachers, including support teachers, librarians, and other professionals who normally did not work with large groups of children, and especially not in multiage settings. The planning committee acknowledged some of these concerns, including "group dynamics, unknown meeting structure, change, working with 15 students at a time, and unexpected change," during the presentation.

Principal Shannon then spoke to the group, stressing the flexibility that teachers had to adapt SSAs to better align with their teaching beliefs and goals. She said:

We hope you see the advantages in this. We're not advising students. The kids will advise one another and help with transitions. We'll be there as the rock that brings everybody together and helping set up those things. And if you're apprehensive, then talk to somebody else. We'll give you lesson ideas centered on tools for citizenship. . . . All of you are such great teachers. . . . We're creating this as we're going. For those of you who need that structure—sorry. The gift of this is that we're creating this as we're going.

At the conclusion of this discussion, the teachers began planning for the initiative that would begin in less than a month. Although the committee and Principal Shannon felt it was important to start the SSAs quickly, such rapid implementation upset some teachers, who felt they did not have time to provide input into the creation of SSAs or the option to refuse participation.

ENCOURAGING TEACHER CHOICE

Acknowledging that teachers were at different levels of acceptance of social and civic engagement efforts at the school, Principal Shannon set an expectation that *how* SSAs operated would vary greatly from classroom to classroom. As a 5th-grade teacher explained:

Even though Shannon said, "This is it" and went full steam, she left it pretty open, at least from my perspective. It could be whatever teachers needed it to be. Because everyone has their own M.O. when they're teaching. It's hard to say, "You're doing this thing, and also you have to do it this way." So I think that she tried to meet a lot of needs with one, because she said, "This is what we're doing." . . . I think that people were able to do what they needed to do to make it successful.

The SSA time was intended to foster a caring environment for students, but would build upon the talents and interests of different teachers. SSAs could emphasize both academic and social/civic skills, as well as student voice and service learning. Shannon explained in an interview later that year:

One of the things I'm hoping that this becomes is a great forum for people to look at service-learning activities that they can do. . . . I don't want to sound disappointed if someone just does community building [and does not integrate service learning into their SSA]. If they are even just a mentor, I'll have accomplished a goal. If they even make a connection, I'll have accomplished a goal.

Ms. Howard recognized that everyone implemented SSAs a little bit differently, as expected: "I know that everyone's take on SSA is a little different. None of it is bad. It's just different. It's a golden opportunity for us to do a number of things." Howard hoped that encouraging teachers to adapt SSAs based on teacher strengths, goals, and talents would build buy-in among skeptical teachers and foster engagement through conversations among teachers in the school to share SSA lesson plans and ideas.

Teachers valued SSAs—83% of Dewey teachers viewed SSAs as important in a survey that we conducted the first year of SSAs. As one teacher noted, "I like the idea of getting to know a smaller set of students better"; another said, "I love the opportunity to form small, cross-grade groups of children." Other strengths teachers pointed out included building rapport among students, teachers, and administrators, which improved school community, gave students a voice, and fostered democratic values. In a focus group interview, another teacher similarly explained that the purpose of the SSAs was "the connection that we're building with students. It is interaction with one more adult that cares in their life. . . . There are far too many students in our school who do not have a lot of adult and kind and caring support."

Though most teachers were enthusiastic about the initiative, 17% of Dewey staff felt that the initiative was not very important, according to our survey during the first year of the initiative. Concerned teachers believed the SSAs were decreasing instructional time and characterized them as "superfluous, not necessary, redundant, and taking precious instruction time away from an already packed curriculum." A specialist teacher further lamented in a focus group interview: "They're trying to fix something that ain't broken . . . and then they're going to break it." This teacher felt that the school already spent ample time on community building and felt that the SSA time would be better spent on traditional instruction rather than on what he/she viewed as additional community-building activities.

Missing from the SSA initiative was time for teachers to collaborate as they did in the Schoolyard project (see Chapter 5). No external funding supported the SSA project. Teachers were given freedom to define their own space, but they had to get started quickly and without being given sense-making time to decide how to make use of the space they were provided. Our focus groups of teachers indicated that the nonclassroom teachers experienced a great amount of anxiety regarding the initiative because they had little experience working with large groups of children, including cross-age groups—especially specialist teachers such as the librarians, school nurses, and reading specialists who usually worked one-on-one or in small groups with children. For example, one SSA leader who was not a classroom teacher pointed out that she "doesn't even have a teaching certificate," let alone have the know-how to "lead kids from kindergarten to 5th grade" at one time. Even a teacher highly supportive of SSAs described the program as "very important but at the same time we must be careful that we are addressing all the students' interests, needs, and developmental levels." These concerns were understandable given the myriad of challenges in the SSA structure.

Teachers also had to take extra time in lesson planning to ensure that activities fit the needs of a range of developmental levels from ages 5 to 11. Another teacher raised concerns that the group size made it difficult to address the needs of all students. Others simply did not want to have an additional subject to prepare for each month. Many kindergarten teachers wished the principal would "put the lesson plan in my mailbox" rather than requiring the teachers to develop their own vision. One teacher lamented:

> It's one more thing—the one more thing that's too much. And the fact that we have to plan [for SSA]. I know that there are [resources for planning SSAs] available but nobody ever does that [plan ahead for SSA]. People are always like, "Oh my god, what am I going to do?" and are searching for something that fits their style [at the last minute]. So it's a stressful time each month.

Despite these concerns from a small group of teachers, Shannon and the planning team discouraged a one-size-fits-all approach. Instead, the planning team used a wiki space online to offer a variety of sample lesson guides and ideas for the SSA session based on citizenship curricula. Principal Shannon also purchased a book on the incorporation of service learning into advisory groups for each teacher.

IMPLEMENTATION WILL VARY ACROSS TEACHERS

To better understand the experiences occurring in the SSA, our research team spent a year attending six SSAs. Aligning with our survey data, we found that teachers tended to emphasize three strategies in SSAs: (1) cross-age community building, (2) citizenship skills, and (3) service learning. Even though the choice of pedagogy was quite different from class to class, Dewey teachers seemed to like the differences in choices and valued the differences as having meaning for the school community. One teacher who focused on building community observed the range of choices by teachers: "Half [the teachers] do the crafty stuff, community, and the other half are split" between civic and service-learning projects." Another teacher who was very supportive of using SSAs for service-learning and student-driven decisionmaking was careful to show the value of the range of teacher choices for the SSA time. She stressed:

> I know some people play games, and some people do crafts. But you know what? I guarantee you that you could walk into any . . . well, I'm making an assumption about what I think I know about kids. But I think that the kids who are making crafts are pretty happy making crafts. Because that's the tone that was set for them in their group from the beginning. I think that we'll probably have a time where we do something crafty, but I need it to be for the good of someone else, too. If we do something crafty, I'd like for it to be helpful for someone in some way.

For the remainder of this chapter, we pull from our observations of these six classrooms to highlight the range in SSA groups. The teachers in this chapter represent a range of ways to implement the SSA. Although they overlapped in purpose, the main vision for each teacher differed—building community through cross-age groups, deepening weekly civic lessons through building shared rapport, and engaging in service-learning activities that strengthened academic learning principles. Figure 7.1 illustrates these three themes and how they overlap and interact.

Figure 7.1. Three Themes That Strengthen Academic Learning

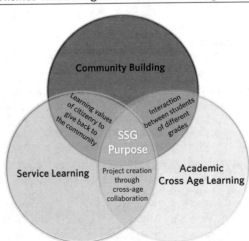

The three teachers described below had a broad range of teacher experience. Teachers Smith and Howard each had over 20 years of experience, while Ms. Silver was only in her 2nd year of teaching. The teachers also varied in their enthusiasm for the SSA effort. Teachers Howard and Silver had been on the planning committee for the initiative, so they were more supportive than others and also had greater understanding of the visions of the project and the resources available for use. Smith, on the other hand, voiced support for the initiative during the August training, but historically she had experienced many disagreements with Principal Shannon regarding the way Dewey operated. Though Shannon and Smith shared an opposition to heavy testing and accountability, Shannon believed more in the ability of kindergartners to take on deeper learning, while Smith embraced a developmental view of kindergarten that emphasized social skills more than academic learning.

CASE STUDY OF COMMUNITY BUILDING: "SO THEY FEEL LIKE SOMEONE CARES ABOUT THEM"

Kids trickle into the room, and Mrs. Smith welcomes them warmly and asks them to sit in a circle around her rocking chair. The older students whisper and giggle with one another, but otherwise the students sit quietly while they wait for everyone to arrive.

Mrs. Smith begins the lesson with a "get-to-know-you" game: "When I say your number, I want you to go to the center, give a high-five, and say, 'Howdy!'"

Mrs. Smith has arranged the numbers so that an older and a younger student will meet for each pair. After the hello, Mrs. Smith asks each pair to introduce themselves and to say something about themselves.

After the introduction, Mrs. Smith describes to students the character value of the week: "Today we are going to talk about perseverance." After a brief discussion about the character trait, Mrs. Smith gives an overview of the main activity—making a craft.

Fitting with her goal of cross-age learning, Mrs. Smith pairs each of the younger children with an older child, always of the same gender. She tells the room, "This is the deal; I want one of the older kids to sit with one of the younger kids to help."

She continues: "Today we are going to make clay animals. Here is an example that I have made." She holds up a clay animal for the students to see.

A younger child asks: "Does it have to be an animal? I want to make the Eiffel Tower."

Mrs. Smith responds that for this activity the students are supposed to make animals. But they are allowed to choose their materials and design the animal in any way they wish.

Although most work is done independently, the students sit intermingled based on Mrs. Smith's assignment of students. There is little conversation among the students during the activities, other than the older students speaking across the room to one another.

Carrie Jo, a 5th-grader, makes sure to sit with Ashley (a kindergartner) during the activity. Though the other pairs of students seem to change each month, Carrie Jo and Ashley clearly have a strong rapport. They stay close to each other throughout the class and pair together without direction as the activity begins.

Once students are settled into the activity, Mrs. Smith circulates through the room. She sets out a snack for each student. While doing so, she talks to students, asking them how they are doing. She projects a feeling of genuine interest in their lives and an air of relaxation about their time together. Fourth-grader Emma shared with our researcher, "I like how Mrs. Smith is really nice, and I like the people in our group. It's good knowing more people."

Throughout the half hour the group spends together, Mrs. Smith calls across the room to remind the older students to help younger ones: "Lawrence, you are going to have to help him, prod him along."

She especially keeps watch over a kindergartner named Ivan, a student with developmental delays. Mrs. Smith prompts an older student to help Ivan complete his tasks.

In this SSA, it was typical for the older students to finish their craft activity first and then walk around the room, some finding another way to stay busy such as playing games and puzzles, even when the younger students are often still not done. "I'll give you time next time" (to finish). Mrs. Smith responds to the younger students. However, because the group meets only once a month, this kind of makeup time was difficult to promise.

With 10 minutes left in the SSA, Smith encourages the youngest children to finish up making their clay animal. The room becomes hurried as children rush to finish and put away their supplies. Students leave the classroom in small groups as they finish cleaning up.

Building community, as demonstrated in Mrs. Smith's classroom, was commonly viewed as a central goal of SSAs—60% of teachers reported that the main purpose of SSAs was to build community. One teacher elaborated on the survey that building community was a way "to allow students, staff, and faculty members to get to know each other in new ways." When it came to community-building choices, teachers who were less enthusiastic about SSA lesson plans tended to focus on simpler activities, such as the clay animal activity. Teacher Smith structured her lessons to focus on cross-age community building, with older and younger students working on a craft activity each class.

A veteran kindergarten teacher, Mrs. Smith spoke about creating a space for students to decompress with simple craft activities—a time where students could relax from the academic work in their regular classes: "We talk and I like to do crafts with them because I know the older kids don't get to do them. And . . . they're always excited about them." For teachers like Mrs. Smith, SSAs provided a time to build community and to create a caring and supportive environment: It was not a time to integrate academics or service learning.

Community-building teachers focused on forming caring intrapersonal relationships and widening community across grade levels. "You can help someone not fall through the cracks. You get a chance to help someone. . . . I'm excited," Mrs. Smith expressed during the initial training at the start of the school year. During the second SSA meeting of the year, Mrs. Smith told the students: "We're going to help and learn from each other and become good friends. So when we see each other in the hallway, make sure to say hello to your small school friends." In between the monthly SSAs, Mrs. Smith would seek out her SSA students in the hallway to give them a hug. She explained: "When I see them in the hallway, I can give them a hug, and that's nice; they can feel like someone else cares about them."

A focus group of students in Mrs. Smith's SSA reported enjoying the space in their SSA to talk and be heard. Carrie Jo explained, "In All-School Assembly (ASA), you can't really like come out and talk and just say stuff when you want to. But in Small School Advisory, you get to actually have somebody listen to you. So everyone can see you and listen to you instead of just listening to the people up there, like at ASA. And sometimes answering a question they come to you, instead of like, because you can actually talk and talk about things that happened."

The older children especially valued the leadership opportunities that Smith provided in their SSA. According to Carrie Jo, "The older kids, like in 3rd, 4th, and 5th grade, go pick up the 2nd and under grades and they take them to the classroom." Fourth-grader Trevor added, "You're getting together with one of the younger kids and you're helping them work on whatever you're doing."

Even with everything Ms. Smith accomplished with building community, she still wished for more. The limited time granted for SSAs hindered Ms. Smith's attempts to build a strong community with her students—both in terms of the duration of the class and the infrequency of meetings. Sometimes the group struggled to complete even simple art projects, let alone build a trusting community. Ms. Smith compared the different feelings of trust that developed in her classroom and her SSA: "It's not enough time to trust each other. Not enough time like in a classroom, where you really build community and you really take risks and you're like a family."

CASE STUDY OF CITIZENSHIP SKILLS: "WHAT IS HONESTY?"

Twelve students gather together on the classroom rug as Ms. Silver and the children greet one another cheerfully. While they all wait for the final students to arrive, Ms. Silver converses with the students present about their favorite things that have occurred during the day so far. Once all the students are present, Ms. Silver asks the group a question: "What is honesty and why is it important?"

Students answer by raising their hands. Ms. Silver calls on each student by name. Students fidget with their nametag necklaces while they listen and contribute to the conversation. They take turns responding. Students Ron, Beatrix, and Calie elaborate on why honesty is an important characteristic of friendship. Another student offers an example from home about a time when a sibling was not honest.

After allowing all the students to speak who wish to do so, Ms. Silver turns the conversation to talk about a book called *King Max*. Introducing the book, Ms. Silver suggests that honesty is a characteristic of a good friend. Ron adds, "If you are not honest, then you are not worthy of trust."

Ms. Silver's mini-lesson on a character trait and a book would usually be followed by a hands-on activity involving small-group work to build community and emphasize the theme of the week. Activities included attempting to retrieve pennies frozen into individual ice cubes to show perseverance, creating a craft project with a set of parameters to focus on collaboration, and conducting peer interviews to focus on listening. Ms. Silver always tried to end her SSA with a discussion of what students learned and how they felt, although the group was often pressed for time.

A novice teacher, Ms. Silver was known for her meticulous planning and thoughtful lessons. These lessons relied on scaffolding of student expertise to encourage cross-aged learning the same way Ms. Smith did in her SSA. For example, when she asked the students to create turkeys without using scissors, Ms. Silver placed students into groups where there was a 5th-grader or 4th-grader in a group with a kindergartner or a 1st-grader in a way similar to how Smith conducted her SSAs.

Ms. Silver designed these community-building exercises to align with the school's weekly citizenship theme, as did 12% of Dewey teachers. Other themes included perseverance, courage, and trust. As described by a teacher in our survey, SSAs could focus on "belongingness and purpose to the children at this school and to learn [civic] skills together." Ms. Silver shared this vision of community-building in SSAs.

A focus group of Ms. Silver's students reported that they had found a space to share their voice and experiences in the SSA. One expressed that he liked SSAs better than ASA because "we can actually talk." Students expressed that the teacher took a genuine interest in their lives and wanted to hear about their day and how they were doing. Ms. Silver encouraged all students to be heard and understood. In the SSA, we observed her frequently asking students to speak from their experiences, including sharing how they were feeling or giving examples of a situation they had encountered.

Ms. Silver said she had also considered adding service learning to her SSAs, but she did not attempt to do so during the first year of the program. Our observations indicated that she shared the concern about the time constraints of a 30-minute SSA expressed by Teacher Smith and she struggled with the once-a-month format. She often referenced time constraints during the ending activities. During the 2nd year of the program, SSA time was expanded to 45 minutes to help provide time for meaningful activities, such as service-learning projects.

CASE STUDY OF SERVICE LEARNING: SENDING BOOKS TO AFRICA

Students file into a half-size classroom and sit in one of the chairs arranged in the shape of a circle. They quietly talk among themselves until Ms. Howard greets the group. The teacher begins the meeting by asking the students, "Who remembers the name of our group?"

Students eagerly raise their hands. "The Seventeen Penguins!" one student answers.

"That's right!" says Ms. Howard. "Collette and I have been giving each other a secret greeting in the hallways that I'd like to use here in our meetings together. Collette, do you want to demonstrate our special greeting?" Collette bends her arm and rubs elbows with Ms. Howard, as penguins might do.

Ms. Howard tells the group, "Let's go around the circle and give a 'flipper hello' to our neighbors." By tapping one's elbow against another's, the kids pass "the flipper" to the next student around the circle. Ms. Howard adds, "When I see you in the hallway, I'll ask you to 'Give me some fin!' because we're members of the Seventeen Penguins Club!" The children smile.

After the flipper ritual, Ms. Howard shifts to the focus of that SSA session—the African Library Project that was developed by teacher interns in the school. The school has been collecting books to build a library in a primary school in Swaziland. Ms. Howard integrates geography, mathematics, reasoning, literature, and group planning into this project. She reviews how her SSA group spent their last meeting together using their math skills to figure out how many boxes their SSA group would need to ship the books to Africa.

Ms. Howard then asks the group if they have any questions about the project. Chrissy asks, "How many schools are getting the books?" Ms. Howard answers, "One so far. Let's learn about the country where we're sending the books." She then introduces a book about Swaziland. Some children move to the floor to see better. One kindergarten girl sits in a 5th-grader's lap.

After the story, the SSA time ends. The group gathers together and gives group "high-fives" to one another. The children form another circle and give a final "flipper shake" to say good-bye. On the way out, one 5th-grade boy, Josh, who had, in Ms. Howard's words, "pooh-poohed" the African Library Project in previous gatherings, comes up to Ms. Howard and asks for website addresses about Swaziland because, he says, "I want to go home and look at the sites."

Ms. Howard reflects afterward that when Josh approached her, "I thought, 'Ha! Good!'" Josh is clearly making connections to the group and developing an interest in participating in the project.

While not too common, 20% of Dewey staff used the SSA time to create opportunities for service-learning activities. Commenting in the open-ended section of the survey, one service-learning-focused teacher said the SSA provides "opportunities to see how truly connected we all are to one another!" Although Principal Shannon welcomed all types of SSAs, she hoped that many teachers would incorporate service learning into the work: "We've got $10,000 that needs to be put into service-learning activities [from an external grant]. I'm hoping that SSA becomes a place where we make those decisions . . . and it's a great place to give kids a room to have voice."

Ms. Howard was committed to the service-learning vision for ASA. One of the SSA, she combined emphases on building community and teaching both citizenship *and* academic skills. She bound these goals in a larger vision of connecting her SSA to the broader world. A veteran teacher of over 22 years, Ms. Howard was confident that she could hold all these goals together despite time constraints. She explained:

> I want us to bond with a purpose. . . . My belief with this is that a lot of people are doing "getting-to-know-you" activities, which is fine. But I think you can do a "getting-to-know-you" activity and not teach. . . . There *has* to be a lot of teaching that goes into service learning. School is not summer camp, so there's only so much time. . . . I value community building, but there's a way to do community building and instruction. . . . We're teaching and learning together.

As the project developed, the SSA students worked collaboratively to sort, count, weigh, and send books to Africa. Ms. Howard carefully determined the distribution of groups primarily based on students' abilities. For example, she asked the young children to count the books while the older children weighed the books and calculated the shipping costs. The next month, Ms. Howard's SSA added public-speaking skills to their repertoire as they presented their work at an All-School Assembly.

At this point in the evolution of their SSA (December of the first year of SSAs), the purpose of the group's work was adult-centered and adult-defined. Ms. Howard agreed with this classification but clarified that she intended to give the students more voice as they were capable. She explained:

> The purpose [of the SSA] was defined by me, [by choosing to work with] the African Library Project, and I think we got into that pretty quickly. But then the quandary becomes, what will they want to do, next? And they'll have much more of a say in that than . . . than they did the first time.

"I only thought the community was important people. But now I realize it's all the people in the world," said a 4th-grader in Ms. Howard's SSA. Indeed, the service-learning project helped the students see how they could make a difference in the world. Their community book collection campaign garnered 10,000 books that were sorted and sent to Swaziland. Later in the year, students sold heart-shaped pins (made by their SSA) to raise funds for Haiti relief efforts after a hurricane devastated the island.

Ms. Howard valued students' input and their participation. She noted, "SSA, to me, is an opportunity for children to find their voice and become involved in meaningful participation." But because of time and preparation factors, Ms. Howard had to balance the momentum of the projects with her own high level of leadership. Students in her SSA shared with us that they were very satisfied with their projects. Yet some students classified this type of work as not "real" school-work. Josh, the 5th-grader mentioned above, said in a focus group interview, "I'd rather spend my time learning something." We noted how service learning, to both teachers and students, at times was a less recognizable process than the tradition-al pencil, paper, and book format of learning. Nonetheless, throughout the proj-ects, evidence of engaged and applied academic learning was clear: Students used Swaziland's location on a map to calculate how far the books would travel; rea-soned mathematically as they counted, weighed, and sorted books; and considered how many boxes they needed. Additionally, they got experience in public speaking at the All-School Assembly. Their collective pride and knowledge of what they "can do together" was evident from their growing sense of making a difference in their community (that is, civic efficacy).

The evolution of this group was evident the following year. The class contin-ued with the same rituals of "giving some fin" as a greeting when the Seventeen Penguins reconvened. But the 2nd year (with 14 of the 17 students returning), Ms. Howard asked the students what projects *they* wanted to do. "But we have to be careful . . . that what we ask children to do is truly meaningful. Not for us, but for them," she explained . She described how she developed democratic processes over time in the group:

> A passion of mine is democratic process. We have to be modeling
> democratic processes for the kids, because it's not that a lot of them sit
> around the dinner table and talk about how to become good citizens, or
> what does it mean to be a member of a participatory democracy. So I think
> that that's really a very important goal of schools. That's why we try to really
> allow for consensus building and discussion. I mean, this is kind of a messy
> process. As a teacher you have to be okay with the mess. It's probably easier
> for someone . . . [who] has had more experience than someone who is brand
> new.

The student-generated list included cleaning up the schoolyard and writing letters to service people overseas.

TENSION BETWEEN VISION AND DEMOCRATIC PROCESS

Similar to concerns raised about the All-School Assembly in Chapter 6, teachers disliked the mandatory structure of SSAs and the speed at which implementation began—the idea was introduced to teachers in August, and the first SSA class was held at the end of September. In focus group interviews, an upper-grade teacher raised concerns regarding ways in which the SSA was adopted:

I don't recall having a democratic decision about doing this project. A committee was formed somehow [to make the decision]. In August, we [were told:] "We're going to do this, this year." So you run the risk of not having everyone buy into it. While a committee of teachers solidified the plans for the SSAs, the broader faculty did not feel that they had input into the choice of having SSAs. In this democratic school, despite the committee of teachers forming the concept, others still viewed the idea of SSAs as a decision coming "from the top."

Another teacher, though supportive of the idea of SSAs, felt the process could have been more democratic:

Well, I think there was a perfect opportunity for Small School. But I think that the ideal and the thing that was wanted . . . took on a life of its own and didn't allow for people to come naturally to that conclusion that this might be a good idea. The idea could have been floated, and we could have taken a year to think about it. I always feel like everything might be a rush. Like we have to hurry up and do this.

Even if it was just, "I have an idea, and I wanted to throw it out there." . . . How could we structure this so that everybody liked it? How could we structure it where, at least, the majority felt that this would work? Allow it to be the first thing that the majority rules on. And if it didn't go, it didn't go. Revisit it in a year. The promise . . . if it doesn't go, the promise is that we'll look at it in another year, and see if we couldn't come up with a better way of doing it.

Democratic process and clear vision can indeed be contradictory. A common and important struggle for a leader is: What should a leader do in a context in which dissent is felt but not spoken? Principal Shannon reflected on this dilemma, which she faces regularly as a leader at Dewey:

[A teacher told me] that people have complained [about civic engagement initiatives at Dewey] but they won't come to my face.

I said, "Well, please tell them to come to me because I won't know. I'll think we are going along just fine."

And she said, "Oh well, they won't do that."

I said, "Well, I don't own that problem then; they do."

The three cases presented in this chapter represent a range of teacher resistance to SSAs. Yet even the most resistant teacher, Mrs. Smith, engaged in the initiative faithfully. Teachers who do not fully align with Principal Shannon's vision stay at Dewey for long stretches of their career because they appreciate the professionalism of the staff and the independence they receive. Although Ms. Smith had many conflicts with Shannon over the course of her 20-year tenure, she explained why she stayed at Dewey:

The relationships with teachers are highly valued. Teachers feel empowered. The principal allows the teachers to be in charge of their own learning environment. Within our classroom walls, we feel that we have freedom. We are all different but we feel that our own styles are empowered in the classroom. I feel empowered. I have had a tumultuous experience with Shannon over the past 20 years. We have a certain amount of respect for each other. I am very flexible, I go with the flow. However, she may at times have some tunnel vision that doesn't allow many variables to be seen. . . . She is a great kid advocate. She brings incredible opportunities. Veteran teachers feel as though they have a choice. I feel comfortable to join in on some opportunities and some not. I know my limits and feel that I can say no to something. She gives us the opportunity to feel ownership. School-level decisions, Shannon decides. I don't think it will ever be democratic.

Even teachers who disagreed with Shannon seemed to support the way she was balancing the challenges of external accountability pressures with preserving teacher professionalism within the classroom and preserving the ideals of civic engagement within the school. The balance between a vision of civic engagement and teacher voice continued to remain a balancing act at Dewey, but in SSAs teacher choice took precedence.

LESSONS FOR PRACTICE

The example of SSAs provides a very different structure from the previous chapter. Rather than focusing on whole-school community building, SSAs provided a personalized, smaller-scale space for students to be known, share their opinions, build community, and link the groups to broader vision of service learning and related goals.

Build trust between students and among students and teachers. Children enjoyed the SSAs. In focus groups, they discussed valuing the smaller size of the group as opposed to the larger size of typical classes. Kids were known by another caring adult in the school. They were also known to other children whom they might not otherwise have had an opportunity to meet during their time at the school. Simply put, SSAs created another space for students to be known and to build meaningful connections with others. Although our research did not study SSAs beyond the 2nd year of implementation, we can only expect that the sense of belonging will deepen as the groups become more seasoned and the relationships extend over the years.

Foster opportunities for cross-age learning. Within the structures of a traditional elementary school, opportunities for cross-age learning can be rare. In each of the cases examined in this chapter, we saw examples of older students teaching and assisting younger learners (Damon & Phelps, 1989). This focus on cross-age learning aligned with Dewey's goals—its basic structure included blended 1st-/2nd-grade (ages 6–8) classrooms and blended 3rd-/4th-grade (ages 8–10) classrooms. The focus on SSAs aligned with other Dewey initiatives, such as a book buddy program in which older students read to younger students. These activities fostered the understanding that students have much to teach their peers. Older students gained leadership experience, and younger students built connections and relationships with older students in the school.

Increase opportunities for service-learning. Although most groups were not yet implementing service-learning activities during the time of our research, SSAs provided a space to do so, and we expect that more groups will become involved in service projects as the years progress. We have written extensively about service learning in Dewey's SSAs previously (Serriere, Mitra, & Reed, 2011), where we discussed Teacher Howard's classroom further in addition to the experiences of other teachers not mentioned in this chapter. From our overall research on SSAs, we have noticed that service learning in SSAs requires a balance of accomplishing project goals and attending to the process of learning—albeit in a very tight time frame. Additionally, given the flexibility of implementation of SSAs, we observed an intersection between the goals of service learning and personal teaching styles, and particularly how teacher- or student-centered the teacher is. Rather than erroneously assuming that all educators who conduct service learning share the same vision, Dewey's experiences help us understand what student voice looks like in the elementary years and how teacher leadership styles impact service learning.

Deepen meaning in "value of the week" citizenship trait programs. Along with many other civic engagement activities, Dewey participated in a character trait of the week program. Such programs have a tendency to be thinly implemented and not given much thought in many schools (Howard, Berkowitz, & Schaeffer, 2004). At Dewey, however, we observed an intention to deepen the meaning of this program by embedding it in the SSA structure as well as by creating opportunities for the celebration of the traits at the All-School Assemblies. Creating time for reflection around traits such as honesty and perseverance allowed students to engage thoughtfully with the ideas and connect them to life experiences. We have also highlighted the ways in which educational philosopher John Dewey offered two meanings of moral education (Dewey, 1909). One is an effort to produce moral people through character education. The other is a way of being and learning in schools that is morally defensible. We agree with John Dewey (1909) by hoping for the latter version in schools in which all aspects of the schooling, including the structures, emphasize a moral perspective that includes the importance of critical inquiry and working to make a difference.

Allow space for voice even in mandated structures. SSAs provided another regular structure for reinforcing the value of civic engagement. Unlike ASAs, however, in SSAs, students and teachers had much more agency in developing the content of the space. With such a strong faculty, Principal Shannon felt confident allowing her teachers freedom regarding how SSA time would be used. This strategy let teachers implement the SSAs in accordance with their own beliefs and visions. This autonomy allowed a space for democratic processes, even within a mandated structure. When teachers feel well supported, such a structure can yield great opportunities for creativity and learning.

Allow staff to support one another through shared spaces and time for collaboration. The SSAs provided online space for sharing ideas, but some teachers still did not feel there was enough support for scaffolding SSAs. The initiative began quickly—only 1 month after it was announced——and without much time for teachers to prepare themselves if they felt unprepared. For teachers who may lack the skills needed to conduct SSAs, more mentoring may be necessary, including modeling lessons and shared planning time to instill confidence and provide support. Perhaps a formal committee to support struggling teachers would have been helpful—especially at the start-up phase.

Allow space for philosophical differences. Teachers have differing views on how to engage kids in a democracy. With differing viewpoints and different strengths and areas of expertise, teachers will conceptualize SSAs differently (Brezicha, Bergmark, & Mitra, 2015). School leaders must understand individual teachers' experiences, views, and philosophies. They need to consider how teachers might adapt reforms and ways to support teachers to help to scaffold teacher beliefs and civic engagement goals.

Becoming a Zero-Waste School

by Principal Shannon

At Dewey, with a passionate group of educators, two graduate students from a local university, and a core of 10 interested 2nd- to 5th-grade students, we started with an inquiry question: "How can we reduce the amount of waste in our school so that we can reach Zero Waste?" This question emerged in my Small School Advisory (SSA) meeting with my group of 14 K–5 students, of whom I am their advisor during their 6 years at Dewey Elementary. We started talking trash and about the amount that we saw in the cafeteria. I shared about the waste tour that I had recently taken at the local university and all of the things that the university has in place. They asked a lot of questions about it, leading to them wondering if Dewey could ever be Zero Waste. We defined Zero Waste as reducing waste by recycling, reusing, reducing, refusing, repurposing, or TerraCycling* items so that every piece of waste can go somewhere other than a landfill.

It is said that a journey of a thousand miles begins with the first step; our first step was to reach out to available community resources to discover how each of them could help us begin our journey. We convened a group made up of our school district's Directors of Food Service and Physical Plant, representatives from the university who were further along the journey of sustainable practices and waste reduction, and the education coordinator for the Taylor County Recycling & Refuse Authority. We started our meeting with presentations by students and teachers about our existing waste-related efforts at Dewey (e.g., composting, placing outdoor bins, TerraCycling, and recycling paper and bottles). Though we felt some success, we made clear that we wanted to do more.

Our best advice came from the zero-waste expert at the university: Start small, "look for the low-hanging fruit," and then build on those successes. We learned that our trash pick-up was a daily event, so we knew a reasonable goal would be to reduce our school's trash pick-ups. We dreamed of the day that there would be no trash pick-ups and just those of organic matter and recyclables. In order to get there, the zero-waste expert offered some data gathering through a university-assisted waste audit. Our university graduate students offered to do a "fresh eyes" tour of the school to identify where all bins were located and the messages that their locations give (i.e., to see where and how waste was emphasized and deemphasized).

---

*TerraCycle is a company based in Trenton, New Jersey, which makes consumer products from preconsumer and postconsumer waste (upcycling).

Through our 3 days of university waste auditing, we realized that during our lunchtime, our waste total was 775 pounds, which included 172 pounds of refuse and 603 pounds of recyclables. We clearly had some work to do. We learned that our largest refuse item was milk cartons, which our county still does not have a source for recycling, at 96.5 pounds; a close second was plastic film, at 75.5 pounds. We learned that our largest "recycled" item was food, in spite of our composting efforts, at 389 pounds, or .77 pounds per student. Our other recyclables in the trash included paper, 7.75 pounds; 1.75 pounds of glass; and 7 pounds of other recyclables. Additionally, liquids were in the trash, particularly milk. We kept in mind that we were already trying to capture plastic bottles, juice pouches, aluminum cans, and compost that included fruits and vegetables. We knew that we had some teaching to do to help with those. We also needed some "divine intervention," which eventually happened when the State College Borough offered to collect our organic materials (compost, paper containers, and paper towels).

During the fresh eyes tour, the university graduate students carefully mapped the entire building. It was enlightening as it showed that there was no real standard location for various bins anywhere in the building. The only standard was that each classroom had two medium-sized trash bins, one red recycling bin, and a 5-gallon bucket for plastic bottle collection. The perception was that the recycling bin and bottle collection bucket were hidden under desks and not quite as accessible, giving the message that they may or may not be used. It showed us that we needed to address this as one of our low-hanging fruits since they were clearly used every day. Again, we had some teaching to do—first with the teachers and then with the students.

We developed a Zero Waste Team comprised of students, teachers, parents, our school's custodial staff, our two Penn State students, and the district's director of physical plant. We believed that the collective wisdom and persuasive powers of this teaching team would take us far. Then we decided to divide and conquer. We had different groups working on different things—labels for bins, presentations, demonstration videos, setting up the recycling areas, and other step-by-step activities.

Zero Waste work has unfolded in a number of ways. We have encouraged all people in the school to use only one paper towel when drying their hands. It was originally encouraged 6 years prior when students did a presentation at an All School Assembly, "I'm Only One Student, How Can I Help?" They shared their class inquiry into the reduction of paper towel usage in the school. They shared the math behind their idea: "If I am one student who uses multiple paper towels each time I use the restroom three times a day, then I use 9 paper towels per day times 174 days = 1,566 towels in a school year. If there are 500 students in our school and each of us does the same then we use 783,000 paper towels!" They discovered that they used nine boxes of paper towels by just their one class and shared that by using only one paper towel per time they would reduce the boxes used to three. It was a great visual. They encouraged the rest of the school to join them. They shared the signs that they had made for the paper towel dispensers throughout the school. They ended their presentation by saying "I am only one student but I can help." It was so inspirational and generated a movement in our school.

As with any movement, after 6 years, a generation of students is gone from an elementary school, so we need to start the learning all over. The signs remained on all of the dispensers but were overlooked by children without taking time to explain. This time, it was spurred by a TED* Talk (2012) given by Joe Smith that promoted "shake and fold." We discovered once again most people used two or three pieces of paper to dry their hands. Students gathered data by weighing the restrooms' paper towels each week. Sharing that data, the TED Talk, our students' own version of how to dry your hands with one towel, and student presentations at regular All School Assemblies, we reduced our paper towel usage by 26 cases. It was pretty clear that at this point all of us at Dewey—not just students—understood what we were doing and why.

Around the same time, our team changed the sizes and locations of waste receptacles in every classroom and office space. The new trash receptacles, now relabeled "landfill" (identifying where their contents go), were smaller (about half the size of the original ones). The recycling receptacles, previously small and often hidden in classrooms, are now large and easily visible. The implicit messages in these receptacle changes stress diverting waste away from the landfill. But we also make our efforts explicit: Students crafted "Are You Sure?" posters and banners, which we placed all over the school to remind us where our waste goes. Additionally, we had small groups visit classrooms to talk about waste items and show students where the containers were now located and where different items go and why. We also stationed Zero Waste Team members in the lobby for several mornings with a table full of waste items and our different types of bins, so students could stop by and try their skills at placing things in the right containers.

Our work was furthered by Dewey's engagement in various programs devoted to issues of environmental sustainability. Each year, we have participated in countywide contests like Recycle-Bowl in the fall. We have also been recognized annually for the past 10 years as Waste Watchers by the Professional Recyclers of our state. Participation in these programs help us keep our eyes on our various goals, as well as provide the recognition that helps others see our hard work.

The 2014 Taylor County's Plastics Recycling Contest was a neck-and-neck competition with several other county schools. We ultimately won the most pounds of plastic recycled, and another elementary school won the per capita pounds of plastic recycled. In addition to being featured in the news several times, we were awarded a recycled bench, compost and seeds to start a garden (which a scout has undertaken for his Eagle Scout Project), and a birdhouse. Our school did not stop collecting plastics when the contest ended. Each week four to five large recycled bags of plastic film has been taken to a local grocery store that sends the plastics to Trex for repurposing. This has totally eliminated 75.5 pounds of plastic film from our waste stream!

This year, we were recognized by our Taylor County Recycling and Refuge Authority's (TCRRA, one of three organizations in our county) first annual Emerald Award. At their banquet, a Dewey student, the university plant supervisor, and I attended. Having Dewey's plant supervisor attend underscored the power of having

---

*TED (Technology, Entertainment and Design) is a nonprofit company devoted to spreading ideas using videos of short, powerful talks.

him support our efforts. The three of us went forward to receive our award, be photographed, and then I shared some highlights of our team's hard work. The student clutched the award tightly to his chest the entire time!

Our extensive TerraCycling program collects juice pouches, plastic cups, pens, pencils, markers, Scotch tape, and other difficult-to-recycle items. We share item collection with others in the community because we are part of different brigades for TerraCycle. In the past, TerraCycle funds have gone to local community service and charitable organizations. Currently, those funds allowed us to install one water-bottle filling station, and we are saving to install our next two water-bottle filling stations. With our 1-year anniversary rapidly approaching, we have saved over 16,500 bottles. Our Zero Waste Team is having a contest to guess the number of bottles that we will have saved on April 1, with the prizes including iron-on recycling decals and water bottles. Our TerraCycle funds for this year will purchase another water bottle filling station to be installed upstairs. Our hunch is that students are not using the downstairs one as much as they should because they do not pass it every day on their way into school. Our hidden goal is to put the Food Service Department out of the plastic water-bottle business!

Our Zero Waste numbers are encouraging. In 2013, we recycled 690 pounds of plastic, 474 pounds of metal cans, and 10,675 pounds of mixed paper. That is 11,839 pounds (5.92 tons) of waste diverted from the landfill. Beyond recycling, we compost organic matter in 12 outdoor chambers and several in-class bins. This year, we successfully composted meats, cheeses, bones, oil, and paper towels through a community compost initiative. As of December 2014, we have had 26,677 pounds of organics collected from our lunchroom, classroom, and restroom areas.

In our lunchroom, we instituted an assembly-line-like system at lunch time that removes/collects compost, silverware, liquids, Capri Sun pouches, miscellaneous plastics, and landfill-bound waste. This has reduced the dumpster hauls from five times a week to twice a week, which we believe could really be one if not for contractual reasons. Our waste disposal bill from $534 per month to $261 per month. Lunchroom waste has now been reduced to wax-coated milk cartons and silver-lined potato chip bags. Truly a long way from the 775 pounds over the 3-day period that our waste audit showed us with the items that we have now eliminated from this waste stream.

All of these successes have been broadcast to the community through fairs, exhibits, and conference presentations. We view any opportunity to educate others as another step to helping our planet. In the future, we will set up community tours showing where our compost and other materials go, develop a waste protocol for outside groups who use the school, discuss more Earth-friendly materials in our cafeteria, and create an Earth Heroes Recognition Program for students and teachers whose efforts go above and beyond the norm. We continue to push each other's thinking and seek avenues of improvement. Doing these things, we are making a difference in our community and for our environment, the essence of education and action for ecological citizenship.

We've not achieved zero waste yet, but we've come pretty far. In a year and a half, we have our school community on board to think differently about waste, waste stream, and its collection. Teachers, students, parents, guardians, and community members have become engaged even in their own homes. It is not unusual to walk into Dewey and see students (and occasionally teachers and me) sorting items into our collection bins at our Zero Waste Zone sites. We really have composted, reused, repurposed, recycled, and to some extent reduced waste. Other goals that we could address are reducing waste from paper towels, plastic water bottles, packaging by our food service department, as well as the refusal of items that do not meet our school's Zero Waste mission.

COMMUNITY AS A SITE FOR CIVIC ENGAGEMENT

No one ever said to us, there might come a day when they decide not to fund public education, or they start to just slowly pull the rug out from under you. You're going to have to scramble for your job and fight for your students.
—Ms. Owens, a 5th-grade teacher

Articulating the connection between democracy, reform efforts, civic engagement, and resistance, this section provides a way to conceptualize how meaningful civic engagement can occur *despite* curricular control and high-stakes testing. It examines ways in which Dewey Elementary reinforced the value of a civic vision engaged with the broader world.

In Part III, we provide examples of both youth and teacher political engagement. The civic mission at Dewey includes space for adults and children to reimagine the current educational and political landscape. Space exists at Dewey to question and to challenge. Through inquiry processes, students are taught how to question authority with respect and in ways that their voices will be heard. We explores ways in which Dewey influenced district policy, influenced teacher training, and influenced state policy.

Although schools often attempt to preserve a vision within its walls, the teachers and principal at Dewey recognized the need to extend their civic mission beyond the school itself. Inherent in this goal is a focus on critique, questioning of accepted practice, and pushing for alternative visions for schooling. It examines the strategies for such influence—the value of inquiry processes to solidify arguments, the creation of contested spaces to preserve counter-visions of the purposes of schooling, and the development of strong partnerships to reinforce these stances.

The examples in Part III bring us back to George S. Counts's (1932) call for teachers to be agents of change in "building a new social order" as we propose some conditions necessary to create spaces in schools that are democratic and civically engaged. Reclaiming the work of education as a democratic, intellectual, and public activity is part of redefining the educational landscape to include more than standardized testing and other accountability measures. Dewey Elementary's definition of democratic practices is broadly defined and therefore includes a relationship between the school and the broader community.

To engage in change processes requires supports and ties with the broader community. As with the ASAs and SSAs highlighted in the previous chapters, community partnerships promoted Dewey's mission. Forging connections for dialogues, partnership, and contestation outside of school walls also helped to sustain their civic actions. Research on educational change has shown that the likelihood of sustaining change, and especially change that pushes against broader norms of schooling, requires layers of support (McLaughlin & Mitra, 2001; Mitra, 2009b). The greater the layers of support, from the classroom to the school to the district and beyond, the better the school can buffer and preserve its mission (Honig & Hatch, 2004).

Dewey embraces inquiry not only within the school but also through partnership beyond the school. The shared creation of knowledge between Dewey and its university partnership, for example, helped Dewey staff be more informed about current research and integrate theory into practice. Partnerships also helped Dewey teachers and administrators articulate their teaching philosophies and create shared understanding of Dewey's beliefs through ongoing attention to building a learning community within the school and with university partners.

In Part III, we describe the role of the community in supporting and contextualizing practices at Dewey Elementary. In Chapter 8, we describe Dewey students working with district personnel to make changes in school lunches. In Chapter 9, we discuss university partnerships with Dewey through a Professional Development School (PDS) program. In the final chapter, we explore parents, teachers, and administrators pushing back against standardized testing.

Challenging District Policy
Through Student Inquiry

This chapter introduces the activism of the Salad Girls—a religiously, culturally, and ethnically diverse group of 5th-grade girls at Dewey who decided their school salad failed to meet their health and religious needs. The girls engaged in a multi-layered process of inquiry and activism in their school. In the end, the girls were successful at changing their school's salad.

Though the effort to change a school lunch policy may be a small matter, it serves as an example of how justice-oriented citizenship education (Westheimer & Kahne, 2004) can be fostered in the elementary years. It provides an example of a way students' everyday concerns can be entry points for helping young people question policy and to learn the tools needed for identifying injustice that they can use for the rest of their lives. Civic engagement may promote an array of social and political ends; however, teaching young people that they have the right, and per-haps even the expectation, that they will question their worlds is a deeper form of civic engagement than what is usually taught or expected in elementary school set-tings. By identifying, questioning, and seeking change within school walls, young people can learn how to fight oppression more broadly than questioning lunch policies. In this chapter, we show how the girls' recognition of a perceived injustice was supported in the curriculum as well as by staff (administration included).

Justice-oriented engagement student can be fostered through a process. Sometimes called youth participatory action research (Kirshner, Pozzoboni, & Jones, 2011; Rubin, 2012), this strategy focuses on student inquiry as a structure for fostering civic engagement. Inquiry relates to justice-oriented civic action in that it starts by asking questions focused on injustices in society. By providing youth with opportunities to participate in school decisionmaking, schoolwide in-quiry processes can offer ways to re-engage students in the school community, increase youth attachment to schools, and leverage change (Collatos & Morrell, 2003; Cook-Sather, 2002; Eccles & Gootman, 2002; Fielding, 2001; Mitra, 2004; Rudduck, 2007; Zeldin, 2004).

Student inquiry processes consist of students partnering with teachers to col-laborate, exchange viewpoints, explore bias, and engage in problem-solving activ-ities (Jennings & Mills, 2009; Lindfors, 1999; Rubin, 2012). Inquiry-based practice is a form of socially constructed knowledge (Lave & Wenger, 1991; Rogoff, 1990) that frames knowledge as controversial, morally provocative, engaging, and highly relevant to a person's present context. Young people acquire the skills to participate as partners in inquiry activities, rather than as "recipients" of knowledge. Framing knowledge in such a context permits students' voices to be valued and legitimized. Although this process can happen at the classroom, grade, departmental, or schoolwide level, inquiry has the potential to teach students that they can make a difference in their world (Mitra & Serriere, 2012).

For young people, student inquiry experiences can foster civic engagement by focusing on the role of people in the public sphere, known as the "person in the public" (Youniss & Hart, 2005, p. 78). Such experiences teach young people how to exercise individual responsibility for the common good (Flanagan, 2013). These kinds of experiences can lead to increases in civic efficacy, the feeling that students can make a difference in their own lives and the lives of their peers (Eccles & Gootman, 2002; Fielding, 2001; Mitra & Serriere, 2012). Inquiry can foster learning communities that engage young people in collaborative meaning-making and development of new knowledge (Fullan, 2001; McLaughlin & Talbert, 2001).

For a group of 5th-grade girls at Dewey, months of civic action began from something as ordinary as the premade school salad but became an extraordinary opportunity to foster personal relevance and connections to critical issues of diversity, access, and questioning authority. Dewey Elementary School served the daily lunch salad with ham, croutons, and cheese. In the case of the "Salad Girls"—5th-grade girls who identified the issue together at their lunch table—the dietary choices offered at lunch prevented them from eating the salad, their usual meal choice at lunchtime, for dietary and religious reasons.

LEARNING HOW TO MAKE CHANGE

Tameka accidentally signs up for the salad and then sits without anything to eat because the salad is comprised only of cheese, meet, and a small amount of iceberg lettuce. She would not have enough to eat for lunch, because she was lactose intolerant. She tries to trade her lunch with the other girls at her table, but could not because no one else would eat it either. Ayesha is a vegetarian as a part of her Muslim faith (meat in this district could not be halal-certified). Haley was not eating salad that Friday because she is orthodox Christian and it was during the Lenten season. The girls share their frustration with one another and decide to speak with Ms. Owens, their fifth grade teacher.

Often, classroom teachers are the gatekeepers in an elementary school; they have the ability to shut down student requests because in most schools, young students may lack the opportunity or capacity to share their concerns with someone beyond their classroom teacher. Fitting with her interest in civic engagement, Ms. Owens' immediately responds, "I am proud of you" as the girls raised their concerns. She assures the girls that they would all work together to learn more about how to improve the school's lunch options.

Ms. Owens encourages the girls to first request a meeting with the school principal, Shannon, to determine the next steps. When the girls first approach Principal Shannon, they tell her that they want to have a formal protest about the salad. They plan on getting petitions signed and demanding change. Instead, Principal Shannon coaches the girls toward an inquiry-based approach that would start with the formation of a question and collection of data to demonstrate the need for change. Principal Shannon tells them, "Let's start by developing an inquiry question and gathering information. How do we know that this is important to anyone else? We need to gather information from the rest of the school. What questions do you think we should ask others to find out if this is important to them? Protest should be a last resort, not the first step." Shannon engages the girls in the scaffolding process by working on forming strong research questions—"Are students concerned about the lack of a vegetarian salad option? Would students eat a salad that did not include cheese and meat?" Principal Shannon then helps the girls prepare a short speech and a PowerPoint presentation for a weekly All-School Assembly to introduce their inquiry question to the 450 other Dewey students. As she prepares for the presentation, the theme of collectivity arose again for Ayesha as she realizes that the problem was bigger than just the friends who were unable to eat the school's salad. She observes, "First, I was only thinking about myself, but then when I started to get more and more into it . . . there are so many other kids in this school who can't have it, because they're lactose-intolerant or . . . because of their beliefs." She summarizes, "Now, it's not just about us; it's about the whole school."

Ms. Owens and Principal Shannon share a belief in the relationship between teaching and social justice. They encourage young people to ask meaningful questions about their lives. They both believe in the value of empowering students but also in educating young people on ways their voices could most effectively be heard. Principal Shannon's shifting the girls plans from protest to inquiry demonstrates a scaffolding strategy of civic engagement intended to help ensure that student voice could be effective in garnering change. Part of this process was moving the students' perspective from personal inquiry toward thinking more collectively and critically about the needs of all students in the school. Through this process, Shannon helps the girls connect their needs to each other and to juxtapose them with the needs of the whole school, including shared needs regarding allergies, religious beliefs, and taste preferences.

By collecting data, students learn how to draw on evidence rather than from their own opinions alone. This process thus moves the students' views as change agents from an individual to a communal viewpoint. Owens began by telling students that their opinions matter. Tameka began to feel empowered through this process. She explains "Okay, I can do this now. It's my time to shine. Here, I'm going to stand here and fight for what I believe in." This confidence in expressing her views was bolstered by Principal Shannon and Ms. Owens and allowed these students to position themselves as agents of social responsibility. Bella, another Salad Girl, explained in an interview, "I think it's important because we're kind of standing up for all those other people who are kind of shy, and they think, 'Oh, I have this opinion but I'm going to be too afraid to state it in front of everybody.'" Madison, another Salad Girl, similarly asserted, "I realized that there are lots of people who never really thought of standing up for it. And we could actually help other people."

The Salad Girls also were learning that they had the right to challenge adult opinions, and that the opinions of young people mattered. According to Madison, "Just because adults make the rules doesn't mean that we don't have the chance to say that [share our viewpoint]. And we all have the right to stand up for them. And they shouldn't say that we shouldn't be allowed to do that, because that's just against our rights." Madison's perspective fits within a justice-oriented view of citizenship and also values young people's worlds in which students can make an impact in the present, rather than merely preparing for *future* citizenship or action.

Recognizing and ameliorating injustices can be supported throughout the curriculum, and a stance on social justice can pervade every subject in the curriculum. The Salad Girls began noticing a relationship between a history unit on slavery and feeling emboldened to speak up, even in small ways, in their own communities and schools. As Ayesha explained, "If people don't go for what they believe, and then if some people didn't go and say, 'I don't want slaves,' there would still be slavery today, and all these other things that people stand up for. And imagine if it kept the same. . . ." Ayesha demonstrated an imaginative engagement with history, which helped her apply historical consequences to her own impetus to engage civically. A curriculum that supports noticing and addressing societal injustices can support justice-oriented engagement in the elementary years.

LEARNING HOW TO COLLECT DATA

This Salad Girls then work with Ms. Owens to engage in the next step of their inquiry process—gathering data. They decide to visit each K–5th-grade classroom to take opinion polls on the school salad option. Every morning of data collection, Ms. Owens emails the faculty to find out which teachers would be willing to have the girls come to their classrooms to collect data.

The girls posed their inquiry question to the classes, counted raised hands, made tallies with pencil and paper, and calculated the totals for and against a change in the school salad.

During their own recess time, four of the Salad Girls (Tameka, Ayesha, Libby, and Bella) enter one of the last classrooms for data collection. They see the 1st-grade students sitting in a circle on the carpet with their teacher. The Salad Girls stand in front of the room in front of the whiteboard.

As in most of their classroom visits, Tameka does the bulk of the talking. She greets the class and asks their research question: "Have you ever wanted to have different things on your salad at lunch? Or have you ever not been able to eat the salad at lunch?" She then asks the class to raise their hands if they did.

After visiting all the classrooms, the girls work with Ms. Owens to understand the validity of their data, including examining whether peer pressure to agree with the 5th-grade girls might have influenced the totals.

Ms. Owens invites all of the Salad Girls to grab lunch in the cafeteria and join her in her classroom on a sunny April day. The group gathers around a work table tucked in the back of the room next to Mrs. Owens's desk.

The girls add up the tallies from all the classrooms, with Ayesha taking the lead as the chief recorder during the data collection. The group then works with Mrs. Owens to convert their totals to percentages of the student body.

Based on these analyses, "We found that over 90% of the student body agreed that the salads should be changed to have more choices," Tameka explains. Libby adds, "So many kids want to change the menu. It was a good number of kids."

Ms. Owens asks some questions about their data collection processes. She also asks questions that the cafeteria personnel might want to know, including, "How many kids were absent when you collected the data?" The Salad Girls refer to their data summaries to practice answering her questions. The group keeps working until the rest of the class returns from lunch and it's time to begin their science lesson.

Overall, the Salad Girls are pleased with the positive response they receive from visiting the classrooms in the school. Haley reports being surprised to learn from the class opinion surveys that "Most people thought that that it would be a good idea (to change the salad), and it would be better because they'd actually eat the salad then."

Ms. Owens and Principal Shannon both worked with the girls in a way that deepened the students' learning while maintaining the girls' autonomy on the project. When developing student inquiry, one of the greatest struggles can be the role of the adult in these interactions. The skills of the adult advisors consistently have been shown to be a critical component in both successful student voice initiatives and successful after-school programs (Ginwright, 2005; McQuillan, 2005; Mitra, 2005). Guiding young people to take leadership in a student-driven project is a difficult tightrope to walk; facilitating can be a difficult skill to learn (Mitra, 2005; Mitra, Serriere, & Stoicovy, 2012). Though collaboration among teachers and administrators can be quite difficult (Leonard & Leonard, 2001; Sergiovanni & Starratt, 1988), partnerships between adults and students can be even more challenging. Power and status distinctions in school settings present challenges to student voice initiatives in classroom settings. Often, adults either perpetuate hierarchical relationships or assume the other extreme and "get out of the way," allowing the students to take charge (Camino, 2005; Mitra, 2005).

Ms. Owens exemplified the qualities of a supportive and strong adult advocate. She created space for the girls to create a common vision and share responsibility for the group's process (Mitra, 2005; Zeldin, Camino, Calvert, & Ivey, 2002). She also established a youth-friendly environment that removed barriers to youth participation (Zeldin, 2004), clarified jargon, and provided ongoing and clear communication (Mitra, 2003). To serve in these roles, teachers needed support resources. Ms. Owens could be supportive of the girls in part because she knew that Principal Shannon will support her in spending time on this work and will help the girls succeed.

The Salad Girls project represents one of the first times that these 5th-graders worked collaboratively on an extended project with peers or otherwise. Madison explains:

> You have people with all different abilities on a team; so one person can help another person with something they may be struggling with. It's not just one person, so you have many different ideas floating around. A larger group size makes it easier to persuade more people, whereas it would be more difficult for one person to convince the others. We can do many things at a time when we are in a team; we can all count on each other for different things.

The girls' range of academic abilities, backgrounds, and experiences guided their understanding of different ways in which people can contribute to group tasks. Principal Shannon emphasized the importance of growing understanding of diverse opinions as a part of the process. She explained, "Students need to learn how to talk with others who have different opinions than their own. They needed to learn how to compromise and to make decisions collectively."

ENGAGING IN DIALOGUE WITH AUTHORITIES

Informed by data supporting their cause, the girls prepare with Principal Shannon to meet the school's head cafeteria coordinator, Mrs. M. In another example of scaffolding, Principal Shannon explains to the girls how school and district decisions work and helped them practice the type of language that they would use to present their issues so that the adults would listen to them. The Salad Girls then request a meeting, not to demand a change, but instead they decide that they first need to learn about USDA protein and calcium requirements that impact salad content decisions to inform how they could take action. The girls reach an impasse with Mrs. M. The school lunch director explains that although she'd like to help them, her "hands are tied," and she could not break from the USDA requirements or do "something special" that children in other district schools would not receive. The girls, although initially dismayed, decide to continue their research and quest for change. Principal Shannon encourages the group to meet with Mrs M.'s boss—the districtwide cafeteria manager, Mrs. Y.

On a humid day in late May, Principal Shannon hosts a crowd in her office. All six of the Salad Girls, Principal Shannon herself, and the district cafeteria manager Mrs. Y. are seated around Principal Shannon's large conference table. Everyone munches on the apples that Principal Shannon always has available in the center of her table as the discussion begins.

The Salad Girls worked on revising their PowerPoint presentation in preparation for meeting with Mrs. Y. The girls worked on it in the evenings over Google Docs so that they could collaborate even when they were at home. Each girl has one slide to present as a part of the presentation. The group turn to look at the large screen encompassing a wall of Principal Shannon's office as the girls make their presentation.

Mrs. Y. asks, "Are you wanting a salad bar? Those are very difficult to maintain."

Tameka responds, "No, we don't. We just want to be able to not have meat or cheese on our salads."

Libby adds, "You could get beans instead of meat for the protein!"

Initially, Mrs. Y. cites the same roadblocks as Mrs. M. (efficiency, equity among schools, USDA requirements), but eventually she concedes that Dewey could be a "trial school" for having two more salad options for children: one without meat and one without cheese.

The girls are pleased with the decision, which they proudly announce at the next All-School Assembly. After sharing the news that the school would now pilot three salad choices instead of one , the Salad Girls conclude by telling the school, "We also want you to know that by working together you can make a difference at Dewey!"

In September of the following school year, the Salad Girls' efforts are recognized during a school visit from the state's secretary of health, nutritional researchers from the local university, and the president of that university. The Salad Girls (now in middle school) take the microphone once more at their old elementary school and tell their story to this forum of school parents, teachers, students, and visitors. The secretary of health responds, "What's really fascinating is you used democracy . . . you used the democratic process. I congratulate you for that effort. We'll make sure to take this story and share it with a lot of other people in [our state]." The girls also learn that day that the entire district had changed their salads because of their efforts. The girls are interviewed by a local television station and featured in the local newspaper.

Student inquiry can lead to justice-oriented citizenry opportunities through a "rupture of the ordinary" (Fielding, 2004, p. 296), which demands as much of teachers as it does of students. This work shows how school leaders can work to strike a balance between giving teachers space to collaborate with young people on their own terms (scaffolded practice) and spaces that demand participation ("the way we do things here"). A climate of the teacher as learner and researcher can open the school community up to asking questions about social justice, equity, environmental activism, and democratic process that enhance teacher performance, student learning, and civic engagement.

Inquiry relies on fostering democratic modes of participation and letting the people who are closest to an issue impact it. Such work can include establishing new norms, relationships, and organizational structures (Della Porta & Diani, 1999; Oakes & Lipton, 2002). To create new working conditions, adults must relinquish some of their power and work to build a tone of trust among adults and students (Cervone, 2002). Without an intentional focus on building relationships, student voice can easily become tokenism. Students and adults struggle regarding power in developing student voice initiatives, including how best to delegate responsibilities to students, how to provide opportunities for all members to participate, and how to resolve disagreements of opinion—especially when adults and young people have opposing views.

LESSONS FOR PRACTICE

Reinforce change through encouraging layers of inquiry. In this chapter, we have presented a case of student-driven inquiry. This was just one of many examples of inquiry process occurring across the school. The case of the Salad Girls demonstrates the opportunities that can occur when inquiry-based collaboration is a part of the culture of the school (Grossman, Wineburg, & Woolworth, 2001; McLaughlin & Talbert, 2001) and when students are made part of the inquiry process.

At Dewey, students, teachers, and whole-school efforts engage in simultaneous layers of inquiry processes. The inquiry processes mutually reinforce one another, strengthening Youth Participatory Action Research (YPAR) and teacher practice. Questions beget questions at Dewey. Through multiple layers of inquiry practice, the process of inquiry becomes an embedded form of teaching and learning, and sustaining such activities is more achievable. Though we provided one in-depth example here, inquiry pervaded the way in which Dewey Elementary made decisions. Principal Shannon and teachers served important leadership roles in encouraging student inquiry, the same way Ms. Owens and Principal Shannon served as catalysts for the success of the Salad Girls. Ms. Owens's class was also deeply involved in the lunchroom rules negotiations.

In addition to student-involved inquiry, teachers and administrators were involved in inquiry at the professional level, and they also encouraged opportunities for student-driven inquiry. In Chapter 9, we will discuss Dewey's partnerships with a local university that situates inquiry as the focal point of fostering teacher leadership through veteran and aspiring teachers conducting research together.

Structure inquiry as a backbone for authentic student learning. While some activities can be embedded in curricula, the questions that students ask themselves are often the most teachable moments for helping students make a difference in their communities. The Salad Girls case provides an extended example of inquiry. Other chapters in this book also created inquiry processes at Dewey, including focusing on sustainability, environmental concerns, and decisionmaking. Questions such as *Why don't we recycle milk bottles in our classrooms?* led to data collection on the number of bottles in each room and a schoolwide classroom recycling effort including a focus on data gathering in math classes. The question posed in a 3rd-grade science class, *Why don't teachers compost their food like we do in the cafeteria?*, led students to implement composting in the teacher's lounge. Asking *What rules would make our lunchroom a safer and happier place?* led students to another Dotmocracy-focused (Diceman, 2013) project. It led to a schoolwide, yearlong inquiry process that gathered data from students, teachers, cafeteria workers, and administrators to rewrite the lunchroom rules so that they were co-created and owned by the entire school community.

Create dialogue as a learning outcome and a part of what civic engagement means. The Salad Girls highlighted the value of focusing on dialogue as both a process and an outcome for inquiry practice that can lead to civic engagement and foster teacher and student learning. In the current U.S. climate, polarization, rather than compromise, appears to be the norm (Hess & McAvoy, 2014). Learning how to talk about different beliefs in such a way that one hears and learns from the other, therefore, is an increasingly important skill (Mutz, 2002), especially within and for a diverse democracy. Dialogue bolsters the inquiry process and fosters a development of discourse as goal in itself.

Principal Shannon believed that inquiry activities led to opportunities for dialogue. Students learned to take the perspectives of others into consideration. Although changing the school's lunch policy could have occurred in a much faster fashion without as much input, the Salad Girls modeled the process of reaching consensus by listening to differing opinions and taking steps to develop compromise. The girls focused on learning how to work collectively as a team—a team with a wide range of backgrounds, beliefs, ethnicities, and experiences. They learned that their diversity strengthened their entire process.

The Salad Girls example demonstrated one of many efforts in which Principal Shannon supported dialogue among students as a core part of the school's philosophy. Principal Shannon's values align with the definition of discourse as a mode of communication that shapes civic life, "a kind of shared inquiry the desired outcomes of which rely on the expression and consideration of diverse views" (Parker, 2003, p. 129).

Train and support teachers to be advocates of youth inquiry. Administrators should voice support for such activities and provide coaching or guidance for teachers and students when needed. Teachers also often need to seek out support mechanisms through intermediary organizations (Mitra, 2009b) and networks of practitioners working on student voice and civic engagement efforts. Learning how to engage as an effective advisor takes practice and intention.

Scaffold student learning on how to transform a problem into a change process. Students tackled a critical issue of importance to them—gathering consensus and raising awareness about new policy ideas, sharing one's voice and opinion even when change did not seem possible, and eliciting people to participate in civic action activities. Upon reaching the action steps, students had to believe that they could make a difference. Their motivation, in part, came from knowing the historical role of citizens who take actions against injustice. Then, the inquiry process provided a guided method by which they could form a question about an injustice relevant to their lives, collect data on the issue, and ascertain how best to develop action steps to ameliorate the issue.

Leaders at Dewey (teachers and administrators) fostered inquiry processes through scaffolding, which helped transform ideas into action in big and small ways. Ms. Owens framed her curriculum around the ways in which citizens can (and historically have) noticed injustices and made a difference (as Chapter 4 also describes). Ms. Owens and Principal Shannon supported the Salad Girls by sharing a laptop to make a presentation, meeting regularly with the group to consider next steps, and making phone calls to set up data collection and presentation opportunities. Civic engagement can grow from mutually supportive spaces for inquiry that attend to injustices.

CHAPTER 9

The Value of Horizontal Ties

"People have found out that it's a place where anyone can come to learn and ask questions—it's refreshing. They know kids are learning here, and what better place to learn than amid the creativity of children?"
—Principal Shannon, describing her school as an integral place in the community for learning

This chapter demonstrates how building partnerships can help strengthen and sustain a school's civic mission. By opening the school's doors to organizations near and far that are aligned with its beliefs, Dewey developed myriad partnerships with other organizations during its 26 years with Principal Shannon as its leader. A university class on sustainability needs a space to build a greenhouse prototype out of water bottles on the school's grounds. A Boy Scout troop builds a bench that serves as an inviting place to sit in their schoolyard. An engineering professor who is a Dewey parent describes Principal Shannon as "open to running experiments. If they fail, it's not a problem. That openness and awareness is what allows input from the community to swell forth. She refused to be overwhelmed by the testing climate. She creates grassroots and bottom-up reform efforts." Principal Shannon indeed was often welcoming another organization into the school for a tour or an idea for a mutually beneficial partnership. This spirit of partnership pervaded the school's culture and curriculum.

This attitude of partnership was expressed by one Dewey teacher leader as well. Ms. Howard describes Dewey's role in the community:

The school is not isolated. We are part of the community. So, anything that impacts the community impacts us. Schools ought to be vibrant places where members of the community come to interact. I think Shannon has done an excellent job creating bridges in the community so that they feel free to call and say, "We have this issue, can you help with this?" and what they are really saying is, "Can you bring these creative wonderful minds of children and teachers and everyone in the school who are committed to this issue?"

Indeed, Dewey Elementary is situated in a diverse neighborhood bordered by trailer courts, low-income homes, and middle-to-high-income homes. Dewey is also positioned near several of the town's grocery and convenience stores, and the town's main street is nearby. The school is not only geographically accessible, but it is inviting for the entire community. This accessibility has fostered a broad range of partnerships that support applied learning and inquiry within the school.

We define these partnerships as *horizontal ties*, which have the opportunity to deepen learning and amplify connections between theory and informed practice (Dalton & Moir, 1996; Miller & O'Shea, 1996). Dewey teachers and administrators participate in a broad range of horizontal ties—from teacher partnerships to the school's relationship with the local university to membership in national professional learning communities. These horizontal ties create new and sustaining discourses that support civic engagement activities.

Previous research on collaboration such as horizontal ties shows the power of developing relationships extending beyond schools to connect teachers to one another—including teacher professional networks and university–school partnerships (Lieberman, 1995; Talbert & McLaughlin, 1994). Such opportunities renew teachers' sense of purpose on educational goals, such as civic engagement. They also can help teachers deepen classroom expertise and develop new leadership roles (Lieberman & McLaughlin, 1992). Thus, the horizontal ties that created and sustained professional development opportunities intentionally strengthened Dewey's civic mission. They also helped improve teacher morale and leadership (Darling-Hammond & McLaughlin, 2011). Furthermore, teacher empowerment and student empowerment are symbiotic mechanisms. The more teachers feel empowered, the greater their willingness to give students voice and leadership opportunities as well (Bauch & Goldring, 1998; Mitra, 2007; Muncey & McQuillan, 1991), which we find to be true at Dewey.

NATIONAL PARTNERSHIPS

Beyond local relationships, the Dewey teachers and principal also have been actively involved in national organizations committed to democratic principles, such as the League of Democratic Schools. This organization hosts national and regional meetings that bring teachers together to talk about reforms and vision for their schools. In 2010 and 2014, Dewey Elementary hosted the League's annual conference in partnership with the local alternative high school program focused on democratic principles. The League's members, visiting from other regions of the country, toured Dewey Elementary and in one session discussed the challenges and possibilities for democratic education at the elementary level. The teachers and administrators (Shannon, Owens, and Howard most actively) participated in the organization by attending conferences and also by keeping in touch between meetings through email communication.

Reflection at these kinds of meetings has led to many new initiatives at Dewey. For example, when Principal Shannon, Ms. Owens, and a 3rd-grade teacher attended the League of Democratic Schools meeting in Seattle, conversations led to the idea of developing SSAs. Ms. Owens described the origins of SSAs at the League of Democratic Schools conference:

> Last January, when I went to Seattle for the League of Democratic Schools Conference, it was Shannon, me, and [a 3rd-grade teacher]. Of course, when you're at a conference like that, you get all caught up in the possibilities. And Ms. Shannon went out for a run one morning. . . . We had been talking about ways for . . . the kids to enact in a multiage-level way. And we didn't come to some conclusions. When she came back, she said, "What do you think about having a meeting with kids, you know, at different age levels?" . . . So the small school idea, Shannon was talking to [the 3rd-grade teacher and me]. She hashed it out with us. "What do you think of this?" And "What do you think of that?"

This seed of an idea led to a large new initiative at Dewey the next year, as described in Chapter 7.

Dewey received recognition from State Farm for its work in service-learning activities. This award included opportunities to visit the other award-winning schools and therefore provides a network of former recipients who exchanged ideas about their work in their own communities. The school received $10,000 to strengthen service learning at Dewey. This small fund of money has served as a catalyst to encourage teachers to develop service-learning curricula. During one of the district's professional development days, teachers chose to attend service-learning training funded by the grant instead of attending sessions occurring across the district. Principal Shannon explains the purpose of this service-learning training:

> They really want us to do something with teacher training and making sure teachers know what service learning is. . . . A good [starting] place would be anywhere that students disengaged from their curriculum. . . . For some people . . . that's their *modus operandi* to get kids hooked and engaged. Other people will do it in their classroom. Others will at least know what it is and not complain about others doing it. If you don't want to participate, fine, but get out of our way!

SSAs became one avenue to encourage service-learning attitudes.

DEWEY'S PROFESSIONAL DEVELOPMENT SCHOOL (PDS) PARTNERSHIP

A growing trend in high-quality teacher development is the creation of Professional Development Schools (PDS). The strongest "horizontal tie" collaboration for Dewey has been its relationship to the local university's teacher education program. This university–school district collaboration, PDS partnership, has created a mutually supportive space and professional growth for the school district and local university and has slowly gained trust, momentum, and a mutually beneficial mission based on the idea of inquiry over the past 20 years.

Such partnerships between universities and K–12 schools provide professional learning opportunities that are contextualized within the school (Lieberman & McLaughlin, 2000). They provide a way to prepare teachers in an environment focused on developing applied theory and informed practice by creating opportunities for teachers, teacher educators, and researchers to generate knowledge and conduct inquiries (Cochran-Smith & Villegas, 2015). Teachers therefore become sources of knowledge for one another (Darling-Hammond & McLaughlin, 2011).

At Dewey, the PDS also provides a natural teacher pipeline of like-minded teachers who share the same values as Principal Shannon and the school's core teachers. The partnership reinforces Dewey's strong philosophical stance emphasizing inquiry-based practice (Badiali, Zembal-Saul, Dewitt, & Stoicovy, 2012). As Ms. Howard explains at a national conference on reforming schools, "Since this is a changemaker organization, I thought we'd start off with what we want to change. We want to change teacher education and the culture of schools. We want to empower young teachers to be teacher leaders and agents of change in classrooms, schools, and communities. How can universities and schools work together to create future teachers who are change agents?"

Principal Shannon describes how the PDS partnership impacts her school and how Dewey Elementary impacts the partnership:

> Part of my job is nurturing teacher leaders. As they become a part of my school, interns become acculturated as part of the community of learners by being immersed in ASAs, SSAs, service learning and community service, our commitment to zero waste, and full inclusion, to name a few. I see how we are nurturing teacher leaders—they leave us having confidence and a platform to become leaders in schools. I have nine previous interns in my school, and the vast majority of them have roles as teacher leaders.

This particular PDS program has received several national awards and serves as a model for other universities and school districts across the nation, often welcoming visitors. This particular PDS model of teacher education has a four-fold mission built on its four E's, as described by Ms. Howard, who recently retired and now teaches in the PDS partnership:

> The first E: To *enhance* the education of all, particularly the young elementary school students in our care. *Ensure* is our second goal, to ensure high-quality induction of the teachers in the profession. Three, *engage* all in professional development—not the kind of professional development in which teachers are required to show up and it is laid upon teachers but the kind of professional development that is individual, where teachers ask questions of their own practice and are involved in teacher action research. And the last E is to *educate*, educate the future generation of teacher educators.

At the start of the formation of the PDS partnership nearly 20 years ago, teachers were initially reluctant to partner with a university, because of the fear that the university might not understand the values of the school and might not have Dewey's best interests at heart. Ms. Howard explains, "Initially, there was a divide between university and the local school district. Neither side trusted the other. Before the [PDS] collaborative began, [it took] 4 years of meetings and working together on small projects to see if we could work together. We began with eight interns. This was 16 years ago." Ms. Howard describes it like a "dance" in which neither partner knew who was leading and there was some toe stepping. Establishing a norm of shared decisionmaking helped to address this fear. Shannon explains the importance of the PDS's "democratic ethos—our structures are flat, we make decisions together. "

Each year, approximately 60 interns enter the university–district elementary PDS program, after interviewing and committing to spend the entire academic school year with an elementary classroom, staying in the classroom a full month after their college peers have graduated. Teachers host PDS "interns" for an intensive yearlong student teaching experience that asks students to abandon the "university" calendar in their senior year and instead commit to the elementary school rhythms and schedules, including beginning the year in mid-August and remaining at the school until mid-June, well past the university's graduation at the beginning of May. The college students even take their own classes on site at the elementary schools instead of on the university campus.

PDS partnerships across the United States have added an array of complementary goals that include, but are not limited to, a focus on equity and transforming schools into learning communities (Badiali, Zembal-Saul, Dewitt, & Stoicovy, 2012; Burns & Badiali, 2013; Senge & Scharmer, 2008). Anchored in an inquiry approach to learning, the PDS is an ongoing catalyst for inquiry practice at Dewey. Each intern participates in a yearlong inquiry supervised by Dewey teachers, who also engage in inquiry processes themselves. The year culminates each spring with the district/university's annual Professional Development Schools Inquiry Conference at which teachers, interns, instructors, and professors share a variety of ongoing collaborative inquiries. Alumni, parents of interns, community members, and other school district and university employees attend the event. Dewey's central role in this PDS partnership helps keep a focus on inquiry present in classrooms and in the school overall. Each year, several of the inquiries which are presented at the local conference are also presented at the National Professional Development School (NAPDS) conference.

Veteran teachers also engage in the communities of inquiry as part of their own growth and professional development. As kindergarten teacher Ms. Smith explained:

> I really do think empowering the teachers is important. They have to
> feel valued, and then it comes through in their classroom, and then their
> children feel valued. So I think empowering them, giving them freedom,

trust, trusting them, helping them help themselves. Whatever kinds of professional development. I love the Critical Friends Group (a group of teachers who meet, share, and work together through challenges in teaching) through PDS, where you meet once a month, just teachers from all over [the district]. Groups of 15 or 20. People bring dilemmas, and we use protocols to work through the dilemmas. It's really cool . . . helping a kid, or a coworker. . . . It's like having a cocktail hour friend group. It's after school. It's a three-credit class if you wanted . . . through PDS. But I think they were trying to find ways to do it in school for professional development.

Unlike in some partnerships in which school staff members feel like they are at the service of the university, the PDS model was designed to be a source of enrichment for the teachers in the schools themselves. This design served as a symbiotic relationship in which current teachers could grow in their identities as change agents, as professionals, and as innovators.

Though the PDS partnership involves all seven district elementary schools, Dewey is seen as the most active and engaged in the program. Principal Shannon views the relationship between PDS and Dewey as interwoven and central to Dewey. An ever-present symbol on Principal Shannon's lapel is a pin of children holding hands in a circle—the symbol of the PDS program. She explains, "The Circle Pin is a symbol that represents our community of learners that we wear." Principal Shannon describes her role with the PDS as "empowering" and a way to "give back" as she utilizes the following Parker Palmer (2007) quotation to end her presentation at the end of the conference on reforming schools:

> Mentors and apprentices are partners in an ancient human dance, and one of teaching's great rewards is the daily chance it gives us to get back on the dance floor. It is the dance of the spiraling generations, in which the old empower the young with their experience and the young empower the old with new life, reweaving the fabric of the human community as they touch and turn.

Because of this deep involvement, Dewey Elementary influences the PDS as much as the PDS influences Dewey. The school welcomes as many PDS teaching interns in Dewey classrooms as possible each year. The relationship is deeper because of the blending of roles between Dewey teachers and university personnel. Dewey teachers have co-taught university methods courses to preservice teachers at another local elementary school. Dewey teachers also take leave from their classrooms to be Professional Development Associates (PDAs) for 2 years—a local teacher who steps out of the classroom to serve as a support for PDS interns in a supervisory role and as a liaison between the university and schools.

As part of the PDS model, teacher teams work to provide input and suggestions on the course syllabi of university teacher preparation courses (science, social studies, math, and classroom learning environments), which are taught in the PDS schools during the internship year. The evidence of readings and practices based on service learning and democratic practices in particular, stemming from Dewey teachers, is especially clear in the social studies syllabus. Moreover, Dewey teachers and Principal Shannon guest lecture in these courses each semester on service learning and democratic practices with children.

Principal Shannon believes in the power of universities helping to support civic engagement work when such partnerships provide opportunities to show what civic engagement and democratic schools could look like. She explains:

> Some of them [universities] are getting better at having more engagement work, but without modeling it is hard to open people's minds. . . . I would want everybody to know about democratic schools. I would want universities to be teaching more about democratic schools, in general. I would like more of the work at universities to be helping open students' minds to thinking about having a responsive classroom, eliciting student voice and engaging students in their school. Not just "here's what discipline is." And oftentimes they [student teachers] don't even teach that until they end up in school and it is modeled for them by whoever their mentor is. Universities need to go back to essential questions like "What is the purpose of public education?"

The stability of the partnership with the PDS program and the shared vision of what they call "Communities of Inquiry" create norms for teacher practice. Combining this focus with a commitment to teacher professionalism and civic engagement activities, such as service learning, has emboldened members of the Dewey staff to think about how this vision can be encouraged in other schools. Principal Shannon hopes to impact the other elementary schools in the district, all eight of which are part of the PDS:

> So one of my bigger-picture goals is that we share what we do with the district. And we shape what the district does for professional development and civic engagement with children and service learning. So, it's embedded as a successful model. Our kids achieve as a result of many of those factors. How can we replicate that in the school district? How can we give teachers time to talk to one another? How can we value them as professionals and quit trying to do it to them, and let them do it rather than have it done to them? They have a way to go but I think I have the superintendent's ear about some of this stuff.

Principal Shannon created a page on the district's website for teachers to share the school's service-learning practices. The partnership between Dewey and the PDS helped embolden Shannon and teacher leaders in the school to find a way to seek to influence other schools in the district on civic engagement and democracy. The mechanisms of the PDS provide a structure by which democratic practice could be modeled. The shared vision and goals of both programs create a legitimizing force to do so.

HOMEGROWN TEACHER COLLABORATION

This PDS partnership serves as a "laboratory of practice" in which to conduct research about effective practices within a working learning community (Badiali, 2011; Badiali, & Titus, 2010; Nolan, Badiali, Bauer, & McDonough, 2007). The collaborative partnership between Dewey and the university has enhanced the education experiences of Dewey students, improved the quality of preparation for new teachers, and offered opportunities for the ongoing professional growth of teachers and teacher educators. Dewey models for preservice teachers the values of civic engagement and inquiry and then handpick the most outstanding interns to remain at Dewey as teachers. Twenty percent of current Dewey teachers first worked at Dewey as PDS interns while they were finishing certification programs at a local university.

One such example of this homegrown model is the partnership of Teachers Owens and Uday. They began collaborating together during their preservice education in the university's PDS program. They both returned to the university to become certified elementary teachers after working in other fields first. They were in the same PDS intern cohort together, and they were thrilled to eventually end up teaching 5th grade in adjoining classrooms at Dewey. They now both supervise PDS interns in their own classes. Their conceptualization of teaching as integrated with service learning, collaborative, inquiry based, and connected to the world around them reflects their experiences coming out of the PDS program.

By drawing on a shared teaching principles philosophy, the collaboration between Teachers Uday and Owens has helped them to push back against curricula and alternative visions of schooling. Ms. Owens explained:

> We co-teach together, not just plan. So we know instantly how each other teaches. . . . We combine our classes and teach, or we'll mix them and split them into two classes, or we'll split them into groups and have stations. . . . It doesn't matter what you give us to do that, we're going to still plan the questions and plans, so that we have kids interacting with each other, and that they have manipulatives and they have what they need. We'll find a way. We'll do whatever we have to do, with what we have.

When possible, they taught their classes as a unit, pulling together students to work on service projects and conceptual units. Speaking about the collaboration, Ms. Uday shows the range of ways in which this collaboration has unfolded:

> I'm on a really cohesive team. [Ms. Owens and another teacher and I] are very collaborative, and that's encouraged. The collaborative work, in my estimation, is absolutely necessary to do your job well. I don't think that I could be as good a teacher without having those. . . . Ms. Owens and the other 5th-grade teacher] are like my significant others, other than my husband. . . . We really need each other and we rely on each other. And we

think with each other, and we talk with each other. And we're constantly communicating about what's going on in our classrooms, how do we handle situations. So that collaborative piece is probably one of the most beneficial . . . parts of what I think is developing in our school. . . . When we were in different schools, we collaborated. And then the three of us [including a 3rd- and 5th-grade teacher who moved away shortly before our data collection began] ended up at the same school, on the same team, teaching the same grade. And it just made it easy. [Principal] Shannon is extremely supportive of that team approach, so much so that we feel free, enabled to experiment with other ways of being in our classrooms. Owens and I co-teach a lot. And even last year, we ran it up the flagpole and said, "Can we do our Back to School Night together?" since we spend a lot of time with our classrooms meshed. And it's that two heads are way better than one. And three makes it even richer. When you have a team that's working that way and is functioning well, I think it's really powerful, and it ultimately benefits the students and the learning that's going on in our classrooms.

The following is an excerpt from our fieldnotes on a Small School Advisory, an example of how Teachers Owens and Uday's practice was mutually supportive and collaborative.

As students enter the room and sit on the carpeted circle, Ms. Owens and Ms. Uday greet and call each student by name or by nickname, give high-fives, and remember details about the last time they had seen each other. Ms. Owens returns to the question that had been discussed in the previous SSA meeting about what they could do with their time: "Remember we talked about deciding what we want to do with our time? We could raise money, do service-learning projects. . . . So what would you like to do?"

A 4th-grade girl, Danielle, responds, "Well, I was in Girl Scouts and we went to PAWS (a local animal shelter), and we just got a tour of it, so I thought we could help raise money and bring toys for the animals." More than the earlier ideas of sending aid to Haiti or putting together packages for soldiers or the homeless, Danielle's idea of helping the local animal shelter gained instant popularity and near consensus. When asked in a focus group interview (February 2, 2010) how they decided on the idea, one student responded, "We did a vote, and the PAWS got most."

In their next meeting, the teachers take the next steps to make an action plan with PAWS. They ask the combined groups to consider what kind of toys animals needed at shelters. They decide to make toys (sock-catnip toys with feathers) for the animals in the shelter. The children respond with enthusiasm to the task and worked in partners (one older student with a younger student).

In the next group meeting, Teachers Uday and Owens want to deepen the work on PAWS with their SSA groups. On Martin Luther King Day, 2010, Dewey Elementary staff and students participate in jumpstarting various service-learning projects. Ms. Owens and Ms. Uday offer to invite a representative from PAWS to come in and talk to the children about their operation. Students get into groups based on their interests.

One group researches how much it takes to run PAWS for a year. The second group develops the All-School PAWS campaign. A third group creates awareness posters to hang around the school. The fourth group makes phone calls to local businesses to raise money and supplies. Our research team notes the sharing of expertise that Ms. Owens coordinated, as well as the much-needed momentum that was gained from this day's activity.

In the March SSA meeting, Ms. Owens and Ms. Uday wheel in two large carts of supplies that had been donated by Dewey Elementary students and families, spurred by the work on Martin Luther King Day. Ms. Owens raises the issue that they had only 10 boxes to hold all the toys and pet supplies. She asks if anyone had thoughts about how they could organize the donations. Many children all talk at once and raise their hands. Andrew, a 5th-grade boy, suggested that they "make categories" of the items. Ms. Uday agreed and explained how to do "inventories." In mixed-aged groups, the children are given categories—food, treats, and toys—and a piece of paper on which to write the inventory contained in their box. Most students get busy right away, coming to the cart and grabbing what was assigned for their group.

The younger children (1st- and 2nd-graders) write the names of the supplies on the outside of their boxes. In one group, two kindergarten girls count cat food cans at a brisk pace, and the older 4th-grade girl who is tallying the inventory says she could "barely keep up with them." The kindergarten girls seemed proud to show off their counting skills. In April, Ms. Owens and Ms. Uday's SSA groups present the results of their project at an All-School Assembly.

This collaboration exemplifies not only the interwoven impact of the PDS at Dewey but the democratic practices in the school that reached teachers as well as children, creating a mutually informing environment. With a focus away from test scores, these teachers were encouraged to think innovatively and creatively about their practice. At Dewey, we found that teachers were empowered to create, envision, and organize their teaching in collaboration with other teachers. Teachers were empowered to co-teach, co-plan, and co-investigate their practice.

LESSONS FOR PRACTICE

Inspire teacher leadership and teacher professionalism. Through working in Professional Development Schools and participating in conferences and professional associations, teachers have the opportunity to take on new roles and responsibilities. The partnerships at Dewey kept teachers feeling renewed, less likely to burn out, and thinking about issues of democracy, service learning, and civic engagement even as testing pressures kept creeping in. It also provided inspiration and scaffolding for initiatives such as SSA and other activities. Teachers were positioned as agents to create curriculum and partnerships, rather than just respond to testing pressures.

Welcome the outside community into the school. Through community groups, university interns, and nonprofits partnering with the school on a range of environmental and civic initiatives, Dewey modeled an example of an organization embedded within a community and connected to global issues. Partnerships reframe schools as not just responders to the state's policies but as an integral part of the community in which people come to ask questions and find out answers. Developing partnerships with the right organizations can provide opportunities for students to conceive of themselves as changemakers, too.

Encourage collaboration within school walls. Attending events together outside of school walls can encourage teachers to foster collaboration within school as well as build rapport and exchange and develop ideas. Training through the PDS program offers an even deeper example of inspiring teachers to conceive of their practice in civic and democratic ways. The layers of inquiry in the PDS model encourage teachers to continue to question and collaborate throughout their careers.

Create new professional and career opportunities for teachers. The PDS partnership and other horizontal ties can provide career pathways for teachers. While deepening their commitment to inquiry, civic engagement, and democratic practice, they can see ways to step outside the classroom temporarily or permanently.

Provide legitimacy for civic engagement and teacher leadership. Through partnerships, Dewey shares its work with others. Dewey teachers present at national conferences and share their work internally at district inquiry events, and Principal Shannon often gives addresses at events to which she is invited. All of these opportunities provide ways for Dewey professionals to share their vision with others and inspire other schools to consider ways to implement civic engagement practices.

CHAPTER 10

Contested Spaces in Dewey That Push Back Against "Accountability" and "Failing"

with Roi Kawai

One of the greatest threats to a focus on civic engagement activities in the current educational climate is a narrowing of the curriculum as a result of standardized testing. When faced with the threat of unacceptable test scores, schools often re-act by narrowing the curriculum—increasing test preparation time and reducing recess, art, music, and physical education (Cochran-Smith & Lytle, 2006; Rock, Heafner, Passe, Oldendorf, O'Connor, Good, & Byrd, 2006). In such situations, reading and mathematics for test-taking purposes drive the elementary school curriculum (VanFossen, 2005). In this chapter, we describe the ways in which adults at Dewey countered the logic of "accountability" and created or sustained a discourse of their own. In critical, feminist, and sociological research, the idea of "contested spaces" has been broadly defined as geographically or socioculturally bounded spaces where contestation occurs for political, social, or cultural influence, and will be described in more detail below.

When Principal Shannon received the yearly state standardized tests results, she realized that Dewey could no longer hide from a system that creates winners and losers with predictable results. With increasing expectations of improvement every year, the school finally did not make the benchmark for special-needs students—just barely. When Dewey was labeled with the failure to make "Adequate Yearly Progress" (AYP) as laid out by the No Child Left Behind (NCLB) Act by local media news out-lets, Principal Shannon had choices to make as the school's leader.

She approached the threat of not making AYP (and subsequently Dewey be-ing at risk of various labels, including the risk of closing eventually) by using the in-quiry process that guides most decisions at Dewey. After a summer of "stewing" (her word) about not making AYP, Principal Shannon was careful about the reaction that she gave publicly to parents and teachers about their school not achieving AYP. Even though the local newspaper had already published the news that Dewey had failed to meet AYP, Shannon realized that her statements would set the tone. She decided to lead a conversation with parents that would turn the focus from test scores to their *own* vision for school. She brought in teachers and parents to discuss the essential question: "What kind of people do we want our children to become?"

Principal Shannon prepares the room for the annual fall Parent Night, just days after Dewey Elementary was placed on a state list of failing schools after it did not meet AYP. The school missed the mark on test scores (Dewey did not hit the benchmark for the special-needs children in the school). Principal Shannon places markers and large sheets of paper on the circular tables in the school's all-purpose room.

Ten parents sit down at the tables. Rather than narrowing the school vision to increase test preparation, Shannon shares with the parents her hope of creating "an open, thoughtful, and respectful exploration of what we want for our kids and our community, and how this relates to the purpose of public education."

The parents form small groups to brainstorm the question, "What kind of people do we want our children to become?" (The answers could include personal characteristics, virtues, knowledge, skills, habits, values, and so forth.) Parents add ideas to the list such as "able to function well in society," "value each other," "responsible and dependable," "respectfully agree or disagree," and "engage in solving some of our toughest issues."

Principal Shannon closes the forum by saying, "Think about the logistics of engaging the larger community in this conversation. What forms could it take? How can we make sure it is inclusive and sustainable? What is our next step?" Referring to her notes to the Parent Night agenda that she writes, "We as citizens play a critical and necessary role in determining the purposes of our schools . . . "

After the forum, Principal Shannon shares that although she was pleased with the conversation, she was disappointed that only 10 parents had shown up for the meeting. She repeats the forum a few weeks later with another 25 parents. Principal Shannon made it clear in her words and activities that evening that she believes parents can and should play a role in actively creating the school climate, not just reacting to top-down labels.

This chapter explains how Dewey teachers and its principal have fought to preserve their voice during the current educational reforms. Principal Shannon created *contested spaces* with other administrators, teachers, and parents that defy the rhetoric of top-down accountability and reinstate a public education that belongs to a local community, encouraged teacher inquiry and shared governance, and created conditions that share authority and voice with young children.

In this chapter, we draw upon the article we wrote (Kawai, Serriere, & Mitra, 2014) about how Dewey Elementary sought to challenge the ways in which the pressure of standardized testing can shrink a school vision. We use the term *contested spaces* (Aitken, 2001; Weller, 2003) as a way of understanding how Dewey challenged dominant social, political, or cultural ideologies that influenced learning and teaching in schools. For Dewey, we frame contested spaces with a sociocultural lens of contested spaces bound not only by *physical* space (the Internet, cafés, and parent forums, in this case) but also by the *social and cultural identities* embedded within them (Smith & Barker, 2000), which include the participants' identities as parents, teachers, and activist women, in this case.

By holding the parent forum, Principal Shannon brought parents into a partnership to form a conceptual space that could hold the vision of Dewey as a hub of civic involvement. She sought to preserve this vision of the school and protect it from the tendency of the accountability movement to reduce the goals of education to reading and math test preparation alone. In the process, she mobilized parents who shared her concerns about the adverse effects of high-stakes tests on the kids' mental health, the school curricula, and the well-being of the teachers and principals. We focus on the experience of one of these parents—Isabelle—to illuminate how Principal Shannon encouraged parents to speak out against testing pressures.

Isabelle is the mother of two boys attending Dewey Elementary School the year it was labeled as failing. Her history of involvement in her children's education started with advocating for her son with Asperger's syndrome. She explained: "As the parent of a child with special needs, you better believe that we have to be very hands-on with their education because they have special needs." Isabelle describes how her son would often express the stress put on him by the standardized tests to the point where he would scratch his legs during sleep, resulting in bleeding, scabs, and scars.

A politically savvy woman, Isabelle demonstrated a strong understanding of how to frame personal experiences within a larger political system. According to state law, Dewey students have the right to opt out. Only a handful of states have such codified opt-out provisions (Mitra, Mann, & Hlavacik, 2013). Parents who wished to opt out of testing in other states could be punished and students would face consequences for opting out.

We highlight three ways Isabelle created contested spaces in response to standardized testing and NCLB. First, she created contested spaces through public verbal and written statements in blogs and interviews in which she expressed concern about NCLB, standardized testing, and lack of support for public schooling. Second, she contested media constructions of standardized testing by organizing social networks to opt out of the tests, developing allegiances with Principal Shannon and university professors, and engaging in dialogues with the state Department of Education. Last, Isabelle persuaded parents to opt their children out of the exams by explaining the consequences of standardized testing for students, for teachers, and for public education.

The following fieldnote highlights a particular moment in Isabelle's resistance:

A CNN reporter and camera crew walk up and down the hallways at Dewey Elementary seeking teachers, parents, and Principal Shannon to interview about parental resistance to standardized tests. For the day, school traffic is directed away from the parking lots at Dewey, and a prominent news van is parked in front of the school building. The CNN team arrive during the state standardized-testing week. As the day went on, cameras capture teachers reading test directions, younger students struggling with the bulky test booklets, and—as a focal point—a shot of two brothers who were not participating in the testing. In agreement with Principal Shannon and their teachers, the boys are engaging in alternative projects. One brother constructs a structure out of LEGOs, and the other edits an IMovie about standardized testing on a laptop.

The news team wraps up its filming at Dewey and visits Isabelle at her home to discuss her decision to "opt out" her sons from the test. After the lighting was adjusted and cameras were cued up, a CNN reporter asks her: "So what's your beef with standardized tests?"

Isabelle replies, "I believe that the tests are wrong. I believe that they're hurting children. I believe they're hurting children—not just my children—they are hurting children across this country."

Reflecting back on that day, Isabelle felt that the CNN reporter's questions were misdirected. Although Isabelle's concerns are personal, she also saw opting out very much as a political issue. Isabelle shared with us a statement that she prepared for a blog about *why* she thought she was being asked the wrong questions:

> The issue is No Child Left Behind. . . . Ten years of research, study and analysis have proven that NCLB has completely failed in its goals. Non-educators in Washington tried to micromanage the education of every single child. And because that management is based on test scores, the consequences have been devastating for public education.

In this statement, Isabelle believed that although Dewey Elementary is the site of her own opposition to standardized tests, she sought to challenge something larger: the rhetoric of No Child Left Behind (NCLB) and the policy's "devastating" influence on public education. In an October 2011 interview, she describes her hope for a "kind of realization, among parents, that we're robbing our kids of their childhood." She went on to state: "We're destroying our public schools, and public schools are valuable." Within the context of Dewey Elementary, Isabelle advocated for parents to recognize that NCLB and, as a part of the legislation, standardized testing, have implications not only for the students at Dewey, but for the state of public schooling as a whole.

After Isabelle saw how her special-needs son reacted to the stress of the tests, she considered whether she should take action. During an evening science fair at Dewey, Isabelle took a moment to discuss her concerns with Principal Shannon:

> I actually grabbed Principal Shannon and said, "Can we talk?" And . . . she's actually the one who told me, "Well, you can come in and actually look at the tests. . . . Parents have the right to do that. And, just let me know when you want to come in. And the week before the tests were given, they're here and you have the right to do that."

Isabelle describes first realizing that not only *should* she do something, but she *could* do something to contest the demands made by NCLB. That one phrase, "Can we talk?" also sparked a relationship with a professor of education from a neighboring university campus.

Based on this professor's work, Isabelle became aware of the possibility that she could refuse testing for religious reasons. She was not comfortable with this option because her reasons were not religious, so she reached out to the director of assessments in the Department of Education and began to inquire about what options she had for her sons. She describes her experience of trying to opt her children out of the tests:

I called the Department of Education down in Harrisburg and ended up talking to . . . I think it's the guy who's the director of the Department of Assessments there. . . . I explained to him the situation with Edward, my other son. [Is there] a medical exception that we can take? He's just so stressed out about it. And he says, "No. . . . I advise you take the religious exemption." And I said, "Well, it's not really a religious issue. It's a medical issue, except, you know, I don't, you know . . . I don't believe in torturing small children." And he says, "Just do it," you know. "That's what it's for. It's a catchall thing. Just go for it."

In this passage, Isabelle illustrates her understanding of the civic process. She challenged the discourse of NCLB by working within the structures that already existed, not by "making waves" and working outside the system. She decided to take the advice of the assessment officer and opted her sons out for ethical reasons, doubling it as a "religious rationale." Isabelle next researched the policies and discovered that although federal law mandates that students take the test, there is a provision that schools will not be penalized unless more than 5% of students do not take the tests. "But, so it was just a numbers game," Isabelle commented, "and you don't actually have to play. And you're not breaking the law." In this sense, she found a way to create a contested space *inside* the dominant discourse of NCLB— expressing her resistance through a lawful, civic act, rather than creating her own space outside of the discourse.

Isabelle's work did not stop there. After consulting the professor at the neighboring university, she decided to speak with other parents at Dewey about the possibility of developing a parent network to support resistance to the standardized tests. In collaboration with another parent at Dewey, Isabelle sent out an email to all of the 3rd-, 4th-, and 5th-grade parents at Dewey to let them know that they had a voice in regard to their child's testing. She did explain, however, that she had decided to take this action after deliberating about the possible consequences:

We don't want the school to fail. We don't want to get anyone in trouble. What are the repercussions of this? . . . Are our kids going to get stigmatized? Will they get in trouble? No, they won't. To work through all the stuff, because, we're not like Occupy Wall Street.

After having analyzed the possible outcomes and implications for Dewey, Isabelle began calling parents at Dewey and connecting with another small movement of opt-out parents locally, including at one of the district's high schools and with faculty at the local university. In the end, nine parents at Dewey opted out of the 2011 state standardized tests. Isabelle made it clear, though, that the resistance was much deeper than simply "opting out;" it was changing parental perceptions about *what the tests actually mean*. In the following quotation, she argues that parents have a responsibility to know the purposes of standardized testing, the potential negative effects on children and the school, and how parents can opt out their children and how to do it.

Embedded in this argument is Isabelle's argument against the idea that high-stakes test scores will help children get ahead. She demonstrated her frustration by stating: "They [parents at Dewey] think that the test actually means something, and they want to see a test coming back showing that their kid is above . . . meets or exceeds the standards." Isabelle explains: "Parents here have completely bought into the idea that if they don't push their kids really hard, they're not going to get into college, and they're not going to get a job." Although "opting out" is a decision Isabelle made for the good of her children, she sees it as one part of the much broader task of disrupting dominant school, state, and even national discourses about the purposes, implications, and influences of No Child Left Behind on public school education. Because Dewey was the largest provider for special-needs students in the district, Isabelle did feel that her child was well supported at the school with its wider curricular goals and broader ways of thinking about teaching and learning.

Indeed, the specific vision of Dewey Elementary and its services is what kept Isabelle and other parents at the school. To teachers, parents, and other school visitors, Principal Shannon readily shared her vision statement for Dewey Elementary. It includes the phrase "meaningful learner engagement, democracy, voice, participation, authenticity, relevance, inquiry, and community," (see Figure II.1) reflecting her vision of a school with civic engagement at its core. In addition to connecting with and empowering parents, Principal Shannon explains how she would like to empower teachers, and how she believes her vision will trickle down to children, too:

> So it's making sure there's a space and place for those things to happen (referring to the diagram) so that we can work together on creating what we are doing, and letting it evolve. It's messy and it takes time but it's really important that everyone feels a part of it. My teachers say, what is this about democratic schools? We didn't elect you as principal. No, you didn't, but I'm your leader (she laughs). But there's a lot of choices of what you can do, and I want you to pass that on so that your children feel that.

Across the district in meetings with fellow principals, Shannon continued to initiate conversations against forms of "accountability" that simultaneously re-empower and potentially disempower principals if they lose their jobs. In an individual interview, she revealed her stance toward NCLB as she described analogous conversations that she initiated in a districtwide principal meeting:

> Why are we letting NCLB run us down a path? I kept saying at meetings, "We're all going to fail, guys." People keep thinking, "No, not us." Yeah, we are. The more the high stakes get higher and higher, we can't meet those. You look at our scores right now. Unless you totally give up, and you believe this . . . I'm not willing to do that. I think it's so wrong. What are they going do? They can . . . ask me to retire.

In this quotation, Principal Shannon not only described her stance on high-stakes standardized tests, but she outlined the extent of her commitment: She was willing to lose her job in order to "not give up" on her beliefs that standardized tests are not the right "path" for her school. Within the school district and among other principals, assistant superintendent, and superintendent, Principal Shannon reported that she feels positively defined by her focus on civic engagement, and sometimes she feels supported in language (via the district website) and through professional development forums that she suggested. She added, "I have many times heard the statement, 'You do it a little differently at Dewey' and that is said in a respectful manner, not a condescending one." In the following two sections on teachers and parents, we relate Principal Shannon's creation of contested spaces against the dominant accountability rhetoric in education to the actions of teachers and parents within the school. We point out ways in which there was much like-minded support within the school. By and large, the contestation was between two competing discourses: one within Dewey's walls and one outside of it, and from educational policy.

TEACHERS MAKE SPACE

Dewey teachers also chose to become activists to push back against testing. Teachers Owens, Uday, Howard, and others participated in a project called Democracy in Action. They participated in a calling and write-in campaign that began in February 2011 and lasted through May 2011. At its largest, the Democracy in Action group's weekly forum rallied more than 50 people at the grocery store café, and its Facebook group had 60 members. After a short conversation in the staff lounge, Ms. Howard began by buying stamps and envelopes, printing scripts for phone calls, and making form letters while Ms. Owens, a younger Dewey teacher, rallied friends and colleagues via Facebook. The group also used online collaboration spaces such as wikis and their personal email accounts to share ideas, related articles, and information on their action steps. The group's members knew this work was not to be done on school grounds or with their school email accounts.

These Dewey teachers—Ms. Howard, who had been teaching for 34 years, and Ms. Owens, an early-career teacher—led ideological and civic engagement activities and raised concerns about standardized testing often at Dewey. Ms. Howard, who was in her last year of teaching before retirement, had a long memory of pre-NCLB, high-stakes standardized tests, and increased national control of schools, and was one of the first parents at Dewey to opt her child out of standardized tests back in the 1980s.

You can say, "I'm opposed to this," but if all you're saying is, "I'm opposed to this," then it's a hollow call to action. I think we have to go beyond and say, "Everything about what I know about education and children is in direct conflict with these high-stakes tests, and here's why. Here's what I'm doing, because I can't buy into this testing, and I can't buy into No Child Left Behind, nor can I buy into Race to the Top.

Ms. Owens, in her 3rd year of teaching at the time, had a desire for her students to experience education differently from the way she had. Informed by conversations with Ms. Howard, Ms. Owens also decided to opt her own child out of the standardized test (at Dewey). She explained her rationale for being against the "mentality" of putting high-stakes tests above creativity and inquiry: "I don't want them to follow the masses just because I'm not looking to raise sheep." She admitted that she cannot "speak disparagingly about this job duty" or you don't have a job anymore because "we are employed by the State Department of Education and we are not protected under the First Amendment when it comes to a job requirement." Thus, giving the test to her students, she relented, was a part of her job duty as a teacher, but she had more rights as a parent, and she chose to exercise them.

The shared activism and beliefs of Teachers Owens and Howard became mutually reinforcing; Ms. Owens was informed and inspired by Ms. Howard's longer history in educational politics. Ms. Owens explained, "I remember Ms. Howard told me a few years ago that she was a rebel way back and just refused to let her daughter do it[take the tests], and I thought that was amazing." In turn, Ms. Howard was buoyed by Ms. Owens's savvy with newer digital tools for social mobilization.

Next, we highlight our fieldnotes from the Democracy in Action forum created by Teachers Owens and Howard largely in reaction to the state's proposed $1 billion of public education cuts. We explain how teachers became social actors who stepped beyond their schools to question state policies surrounding standardized testing. To avoid political backlash, teachers had to physically leave the school grounds and conduct such activities elsewhere:

> The café in a local grocery store buzzed with collective productivity. A small construction paper sign sat on the central table with the name of the group: "Democracy in Action." Twenty people (teachers, parents, and community members) were writing letters to state elected officials; some were on their cellphones armed with a script to tell the governor's office that money must be put into traditional public schools, not charter schools since charter schools created a large financial burden on local school districts. They weaved in various educational issues to their scripts, such as the emphasis on testing and the value of local control of schools. Owens asked one participant if she was "on Facebook" and if she'd like to be connected to their corresponding Facebook group.

Despite the separateness of the digital, teacher's lounge, and café spaces, the data suggest that participating teachers did not see these spaces as disconnected from their teaching duties. Rather, as Ms. Owens explained, they were all "part of being a good teacher." Still, the teachers maneuvered the spaces strategically with

off-school sites and email accounts that separated their different roles as teachers
and as activists. Principal Shannon advised them to do this as a tactic; her help
served as a measure of her support.

Ms. Owens further explained her commitment to civic engagement and public education in an individual interview: "No one ever said to us, there might come
a day when they decide not to fund public education, or they start to just slowly
pull the rug out from under you. You're going to have to scramble for your job,
and fight for your students." Although she was often cynical about the possibility
of making structural changes at the state or national level, she began to wonder as
the group grew, "I'm making contact with people who ultimately, I think, will raise
enough of a ruckus. If we all stick together, we might be able to do something."

One of Ms. Howard's closest intellectual and political confidants was Principal
Shannon, who briefly stepped in at the end of one of the largest Democracy in
Action forums to ask how many people attended. Although Shannon did not
feel her job as principal allowed her to participate directly in the activities that
were happening at the café, she presented herself briefly at some of the events and
shared her encouragement quietly before leaving. While also monitoring distinct
spaces as a civic agent and an agent of the state, she supported the teachers' work in
indirect ways, such as by sharing like-minded news and academic readings about
testing, budget cuts, and educational issues.

Ms. Howard, with 20-plus years of experience under her belt, remained passionate but unsurprised about the state of education that she saw "coming down
the pike since their first mandated test in the 1980s." Here, she describes her role
with the Democracy in Action group:

> I've had amazing experiences in my 38 years as a public school teacher, and
> I've had the opportunity to really develop these relationships with different
> people on campus, and different people through our country who are in
> the education community. . . . Really, I tried to get people involved. "Come,
> we're going to [the supermarket that housed the café]; we're going to make
> calls. It's really easy." I certainly didn't mind speaking on behalf of the group
> several times, because I probably feel a little bit more comfortable speaking
> than some of the other members of the Democracy in Action group.

The ease and practicality of their civic engagement work functioned by by-
passing conflicting spaces and expectations of the school and civic life. To function with agency, these women utilized and created new and innovative spaces
to engage civically, often remaining what mattered. Parents, teachers, and administration alike, but in different ways, sidestepped spaces in which they had less
agency (Administering the standardized text, newspaper publishing of Dewey not
making AYP) and created a new discourse that mattered to them. Their collective
and overlapping actions were mutually strengthening to the climate, identity, and
ethos of this democratic school.

LESSONS FOR PRACTICE

Recognize that the personal experiences of teachers create a foundation for their practice and how they identify their role as a teacher. In this case, the Dewey teachers defined their role as extending beyond the school to interact in public spheres about the purposes of schooling. For these teachers, personal experiences with conflict shaped a willingness to pursue political activity. When we considered why the teachers, parents, and Principal Shannon sought to push against the tide of accountability, we found that the women we speak of in this chapter were supported in creating contested spaces by making meaning of personal conflicts in the context of systems of inequity and oppression built into American society. As the personal is often political is dialectical (Freire, 2000), we see how political awareness supported their motivation to take action. Each woman cited meaningful and personal moments in her past that shaped her calls to action. Isabelle's son had special needs, and Ms. Owens and Ms. Howard's children were slated to take the standardized tests. Action was inspired by their desire to create a safety buffer—much as Principal Shannon tried to do for her whole school—around those they wanted to protect against educational demands they opposed. As Isabelle spoke of her despair when her son was scratching himself until he bled because of his anxiety over the standardized tests, Teachers Howard and Owens added their own stories about their philosophy of education becoming even stronger for them in their role as parents, forcing them to take action.

In our conversations with these women, all of them described ways in which their family history, in particular, informed and motivated them to contest policy. Ms. Howard grew up in the 1960s in Washington, DC, and cited the supportive role of her father in particular, who framed issues of social justice and democracy for her from a young age. Isabelle and Principal Shannon had similar role models for action and for "not being intimidated by authority" (quotation by Isabelle). Ms. Owens, on the other hand, was taught to obey and decided that she would raise her children differently, and now she teaches her students differently, too. All made meaning of their personal experiences with conflict, which supported both their skills and impetus for contesting policies they opposed. As we visualize the scaffolding or walls being leadership and collegial supports, we see how these women's identities give internal shape, like air, to their experiences of contestation.

Create contested spaces to intentionally support activism. Schools must actively create spaces to preserve the democratic and civic purpose of schools. While the adults in Dewey used their own skills and unique identities and concerns to contest, it is crucial to point out that they created contested spaces largely within the discourse of NCLB in language (opting out for "religious" reasons) and mainstream civic processes (calling and writing congressional representatives, making a Facebook group) and did not see themselves as "rebellious."

Still, the contested spaces occurring around Dewey Elementary that back civic and political action were mutually supportive, providing fertile ground for recurrent and aligned thought and action. We see how these actions occurred within a web of social capital—intellectual resources utilized by participants to reclaim their elementary school as not failing. Dewey created an environment that welcomes change and enables progress within buffered geographical and ideological spaces—including human and informal digital social networks.

We are also aware that some schools seeking opt-out provisions for students are not acting in the best interest of students but instead are trying to subvert school failures. Some schools at risk have misled students into not taking the test in order to hide school flaws. We are not talking about such schools in this book. Dewey Elementary is the kind of school we hope our own children could attend. The school pushes back against inflexible laws that are harming good schools even as they to identify troubled ones.

Help teachers balance activism with professional-preservation. The arguments in favor of opting out and protesting the system must be held in balance with local consequences to teachers and to schools. The teachers in this chapter positioned themselves as agents of change and as public intellectuals who were engaged in collective and critical work (Mirra & Morrell, 2011). Yet, teachers can face real dangers, such as tenure termination or judgment from administration, when they speak or act politically. Teachers in more tenuous positions especially must weigh the merits of perilous activism with their need for job security and their choice of what is worth the fight. In addition to the safety buffer they received in the form of their principal, Dewey teachers worked hard to keep their teaching roles and their activist roles separate. They used different spaces to speak as citizens and parents in the public sphere rather than in their role as "teacher."

We wonder how schools and teacher education programs can develop supportive collegial networks that help teachers go beyond being mere transmitters of standardized content knowledge and toward becoming creators of experiences and knowledge. Practically speaking, perhaps supporting teacher inquiry and teachers' membership in local and national affiliations can buoy innovation and action. Dialogue and collaboration can put educational constituencies in better contact, supporting the professionalism of teachers as well as democratic processes, and better uniting spaces for teachers to act as "civic agents" and as "agents of the state." Indeed, Mirra and Morrell (2011) identify a link between teachers viewing themselves as professionals and civic agents and their promotion of civic experiences for their students. Teachers, who often feel it may be inefficacious to resist the high-stakes testing culture, might consider the problems they face in their classrooms within the context of a larger political or social system. If teachers find ways to enact identities as empowered civic agents and public intellectuals willing to stand up for innovation, they will be more apt to help students connect to their own sense of civic agency, and expand the curriculum when policy is calling for constraint.

CHAPTER 11

Conclusion
Making Civic Engagement Work

Dewey Elementary aligns with a new vision of civic education that emphasizes the importance of critical inquiry for social action. We define this process as noticing little and large injustices, asking meaningful questions, collecting strong data, and taking steps to be changemakers. Civic engagement at Dewey included not just classroom or school activities, but also a responsibility to the broader world. Environmental stewardship was an ongoing connective theme through activities such as committing to a zero-waste goal, lunchroom composting, classroom recycling, and integrating environmental principles into the civics, math, science, and language arts curriculums.

The school had the benefit of a longtime leader who believed deeply in civic engagement. Principal Shannon championed efforts to engage students meaningfully and buffered the school from district and state pressures. During times of change and challenge to schools, strong leadership matters. A school leader sets the tone by creating and shifting the discourses that guide the school (Copeland, 2003). Principals can translate top-down mandates in ways that maintain the philosophical integrity of a school, creating a clear and confident direction. In particular, schools need principals who regularly read, learn, and share their knowledge and confidence with others (Brezicha, Bergmark, & Mitra, 2015). Yet, in this concluding chapter, we consider the lessons learned about Dewey that go beyond the value of a single great leader.

As we reflect on the lessons learned from the Dewey story, we explore crosscutting themes behind civic engagement at Dewey. We focus on the importance of the intersection of student voice and critical inquiry as the central framework that structures civic engagement at Dewey. We then consider conditions and factors that support this framework, including empowering teachers, fostering a climate of trust, and embedding civic engagement in structures and partnerships.

STUDENT VOICE AND INQUIRY— BUILDING BLOCKS FOR CIVIC AGENCY

We view the intersection of *student voice* and *critical inquiry* as central to Dewey's ability to play a role in addressing injustices in its environment (see Figure 11.1).

Figure 11.1. Conceptual Framework

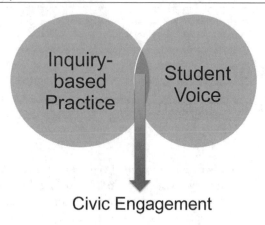

Though inquiry processes can be reactionary and can preserve the status quo, empowering young people to be change agents and providing them with the tools of the inquiry process can lead to civic action in the classroom, the school, and the broader community. One goal in civic engagement at Dewey was to foster a greater overlap in these concepts. Indeed, student voice alone could easily be considered hollering or disrespect, whereas inquiry without the perspective of students themselves can lead to incomplete information. Critical inquiry and student voice together fostered mutually supportive spaces for civic engagement.

STUDENT VOICE AS CIVIC AGENCY

Dewey was unlike most schools in that its approach to civic engagement put students at the center, rather than on the margins. Dewey's 5th-graders were in charge of the weekly All-School Assembly. Third-graders changed the composting policy. Encouraging students to connect personally relevant real-world issues with their own community translated an outward focus into classroom curricula in Stacey Benson's work with her class on homelessness and Ms. Owen's work on zines. Teachers also were supported in questioning testing policy and considering the place of Dewey in the broader education policy landscape. By modeling ways for young people to challenge and question authority, young people learned how to critique and to take action. The focus on making a difference (Mitra & Serriere, 2012a) at Dewey also emphasized ways to question authority in ways that could be heard more effectively in the current political climate, such as Shannon's coaching of the Salad Girls to use data to frame an inquiry to make arguments instead of boycotts and protest.

This focus on student voice aligns with research discussing the ways in which young people and adults addressed problems at Dewey, in which students are only allowed to assume leadership roles in change efforts in rare cases (Fielding, 2001; Mitra, 2005). Dewey's story aligns with previous research on student voice that shows young people can serve as a catalyst for classroom change, such as improvements in instruction, curriculum, teacher–student relationships (Daniels & McCombs, 2001; McIntyre & Rudduck, 2007), and assessment systems (Collatos & Morrell, 2003; Fielding, 2001). Student voice affects schoolwide change, including school climate (Galloway, Pope, & Osberg, 2007; Mitra, 2001), school evaluation (Yonezawa & Jones, 2007), and visioning and strategic planning (Eccles & Gootman, 2002; Zeldin, 2004). Student voice also influences community change, such as teacher preparation (Cook-Sather, 2002), school reconstitution (Kirshner, 2008), and testing policies (Ginwright, Noguera, & Cammarota, 2006).

As demonstrated perhaps most dramatically in the story of the Salad Girls, student voice represents a diverse range of student experiences. Rather than speaking from a monolithic viewpoint, student voice includes awareness of difference and disagreement within groups as well as between groups. It involves processes of dialogue and deliberation to find common ground and to articulate points of disagreement. In this way, as with any democratic process, student voice is strengthened through diversity. Diverse and critical student voice involves a sociocultural relationship between different ways to take action and a group's own contexts and differing beliefs.

CRITICAL INQUIRY

Critical inquiry served as the primary scaffolding mechanism for structuring civic engagement at Dewey Elementary. Bolstered by ongoing professional development and teacher education in partnership with the local university, Dewey modeled a practice of asking critical questions, gathering data, reflection, and action as a process for how to conduct civic engagement. Inquiry at Dewey served a purpose—a goal of making a difference and striving toward a more equitable world. Layers of inquiry supported one another as teachers engaged in inquiries on environmental stewardship, social justice, and student-driven change. In parallel, student questions sparked schoolwide initiatives (such as composting and recycling).

Research examining student inquiry includes scholarship on Youth Participatory Action Research (YPAR). Focusing primarily on young people at the high school level, and in some cases at the middle school level, YPAR emphasizes the value of youth as co-researchers in partnership with adults (Nygreen, Ah Kwon, & Sánchez, 2006). Previous research in this area demonstrates how inquiry processes position young people as knowledge producers who can be engaged in complex intellectual tasks (Cammarota & Fine, 2008; Cook-Sather, 2002; Rubin & Jones, 2007).

The experiences of Dewey demonstrate that younger children also have the skills, ability, and desire to make a difference in their lives, their school, and their communities. Rather than just working on becoming adults, younger children already have the ability to engage in personally relevant and critical inquiry that can make a difference in the broader world (Mayes, Mitra, Serriere, forthcoming; Osler & Starkey, 2005). By engaging in critical inquiry processes, students can explore the world around them, question injustices, and impact their surroundings (Levinson, 2012).

Dewey Elementary highlights the emergent nature of critical inquiry, including the importance of embracing inquiry as it arises from teacher and student questions. For example, we explored Ms. Jones's class of students wondering why teachers did not compost in the teacher's lounge and the Salad Girls wondering why school lunches did not meet the needs of all the school's students. This work shows how strong civic engagement initiatives often have layers of inquiry processes that incorporate the work of students, teachers, and administrators. We considered how to scaffold learners who were new to the process and to value deliberation as a part of the process, such as we saw in the examples of the Salad Girls, the zine projects in Ms. Owens's class, and the philosophical dialogues that occurred in kindergarten classes.

We have demonstrated the importance of preserving public spaces for the celebration of the inquiry work. Through All-School Assemblies, Dewey showed the value of civic engagement activities. Weekly presentations modeled and shared the excellent work that was happening in classrooms, in SSAs, and in schoolwide activities. The assemblies also reinforced to students the value of their work and amplified its importance both to the students themselves and to their teachers and peers.

Dewey's willingness to push back against accountability pressures emerged out of its critical inquiry stance. The more a school engages in an inquiry process, the better school actors become at acquiring new information and creating new knowledge for the community. The assimilation of new knowledge builds on prior knowledge within the school (Cohen & Levinthal, 1990). Therefore, developing an inquiry stance can prepare schools to assimilate ideas and concepts when they are presented. It also encourages schools to become more thoughtful about how to seek the information they need to continue learning and improving practice (Brown & Duguid, 2000). By encouraging critical questioning and collaboration of diverse actors, capacity and willingness to challenge and question spaces outside of school can build as well and help form alternative frames of schooling (Benford & Snow, 2000; Gahan & Pekarek, 2013).

EMPOWERING TEACHERS

Dewey's experience also amplifies the importance of valuing teacher leadership and professionalism as a cornerstone of civic engagement practices. Previous research has lamented the struggle over *how* to engage students as active partners in school change (Cook-Sather, 2002; Mitra, 2005; Zeldin, Camino, & Mook, 2005). Adults involved in such efforts must provide *active support for student involvement*, including establishing norms of respect and equality (Camino

& Zeldin, 2002) while providing encouragement for youth participation (Einspruch & Wunrow, 2002). Taking this perspective even further, the idea of "radical collegiality" (Fielding, 2001) connects student participation in school reform with the increasing research on shifts in teacher professionalism. The concept of radical collegiality is built on the assumption that learning is improved and enabled by give-and-take encounters with their students. That is, communication not only needs to happen from teacher to student, but also from student to teacher. Teaching then becomes more open and reciprocal in nature to best serve the needs of students and to more effectively improve both teaching and learning.

To engage in democratic practices and to develop professional learning communities (via inquiry), teachers need to be empowered themselves so they can help empower others (Bauch & Goldring, 1998; Muncey & McQuillan, 1991). The teachers at Dewey collaborated regularly on civic engagement initiatives, such as the Schoolyard project. Inherent in these initiatives was the value attributed to collaboration and the belief that teachers were the experts; true reform involves giving time and space for expertise to shine. The Schoolyard project recognized teachers as experts, leaders, and contributors to a reform initiative. The Small School Advisory model, however, was less successful in empowering teachers and at leading to powerful opportunities for students to learn how to make a difference. A range of teacher beliefs and experiences within an effort led to varying conceptions of civic engagement in those activities. Therefore, we add to the ideal of radical collegiality (Fielding, 2001) by emphasizing the importance of meaningful teacher-to-teacher relationships as much as between teachers and administrators or teachers and students.

Across initiatives, teachers who wanted to take the idea to create new efforts were encouraged, as was the case when Ms. Owens developed zines. Additionally, through schoolwide structures, Principal Shannon often encouraged teacher professionalism and independence in choosing how to marry teacher expertise with civic engagement goals, such as in the Schoolyard project and All-School Assemblies. Other efforts such as Small School Advisories did not provide enough time for planning, collaboration, and scaffolding. Though less successful overall, many teachers were able to integrate their teaching philosophy with SSAs.

At a time in which teachers must reconcile their competing roles as "agents of the state" who must administer tests and respond to mandates while also seeking to become "civic agents" for a better educational system (Mirra & Morrell, 2011), collaborative teacher inquiry creates opportunities for teachers to embolden their teaching practice from the driver's seat, rather than passively responding to top-down testing efforts or a mandated curriculum. Having administrators position and support teachers as agents of change and public intellectuals involves collective and critical work. Working alongside a university that values teacher inquiry and collaborating was one way in which the teachers at Dewey found and created spaces to amplify their professional voice and engagement. However, most teachers nationwide are wary of how much they can voice their own viewpoints.

Many face real dangers at other schools—of tenure termination or judgment from administration—when they speak or act politically. In addition to the buffering they received from their principal, several teachers at Dewey protected their jobs by keeping their roles separate (although united philosophically) and navigating the two roles with savvy. We wonder how schools and teacher education programs can coalesce to develop supportive collegial networks—networks that can help teachers go beyond being mere transmitters of standardized content knowledge and toward becoming agentic creators of authentic learning experiences.

CREATING A CLIMATE OF TRUST AND COMMUNITY

Innovation requires a space for risk taking and mistakes. To engage in innovative civic engagement, Dewey needed to build on a climate of trust among teachers, students, and administrators. The process for fostering this trust included the creation of a learning community—a way of structuring the school that encouraged collaboration for the purpose of meaning-making and to develop and assimilate new knowledge (Fullan, 2001; McLaughlin & Talbert, 2001). At Dewey, the careful building of a relationship with the Professional Development School at the local university is one model of building trust through the creation of a learning community, including hiring new teachers out of this program so that they began their careers at Dewey already enmeshed in the values of civic engagement, critical inquiry, and collaboration.

Dewey demonstrates the way that inquiry-based practice is a process of *collective meaning-making* as teachers and students engage in iterative questioning of their school practices and of the broader policy climate. Inquiry-based practice is a form of acknowledging and creating socially constructed knowledge (Greeno & MMAP, 1998; Lave & Wenger, 1991; Rogoff, 1994; Wenger, 1998). This form of group processing frames knowledge as highly relevant to a person's present context. Such an approach holds that knowledge is controversial, morally provocative, engaging, and must be personally relevant in order to be deemed worthwhile. This complexity makes it difficult to replicate the conditions at Dewey; however, we are often reminded in our research, teaching, and at conferences that public schools across the United States share not only struggles and challenges but also common possibilities within the current political landscape.

Throughout this book, we have seen clearly how the sociocultural conditions in which civic engagement occurs impact the quality of the school climate. Specifically, it is useful to examine the interplay between individuals in the school community as a way to foster meaning-making. We can see this recurring theme at Dewey within the simple process of valuing diverse students' opinions, questions, and beliefs. We explored ways for adults to foster dialogue, scaffold discussions, and model critical reflection, such as kindergartners getting involved in philosophical dialogues, 2nd-graders learning about homelessness, and the 5th-grade Salad Girls pushing for district changes to the lunch policy.

EMBEDDING CIVIC ENGAGEMENT INTO STRUCTURES, PROCESSES, AND PARTNERSHIPS

This book demonstrates the importance of preserving public spaces for sharing and celebrating the work of inquiry. Through All School Assemblies, Dewey supported the public value of civic engagement activities, and simultaneously modeled it for students and teachers who may soon follow in action. Weekly presentations modeled and shared the diverse ways civic engagement could occur in classrooms, school advisories, and schoolwide activities. It also reinforced the value of the students' civic engagement projects and amplified the importance of it to them, their teachers, and peers.

We found that collective meaning-making is established and then reified through rituals and structures. Through the chapters in this book, it has become clear how supports and structure have enabled Dewey Elementary to be successful in fostering civic engagement. Although examining the mechanisms and supports can lead to civic action that makes a difference, Dewey's experiences showed that it is also crucial to consider the broader contexts and conditions of support in which specific civic engagement initiatives occur. Although they may not be precisely replicable in context, the structures created by Dewey could help enable successful civic engagement initiatives at other schools as well.

Dewey created intentional spaces to make sure students were known and cared for, at social, civic, and academic levels. The school itself became a living laboratory for practicing civic action through environmental projects and community initiatives. Classroom protocols and curriculum content explicitly discussed the importance of care, respect, and justice.

Dewey also showed how embedding civic goals into the core of the curriculum can help sustain civic practice in the face of accountability pressures, such as the homelessness unit in the 2nd grade. At the school level, students were encouraged to take leadership roles in multiple ways by developing inquiry processes from student questions and by fostering diverse student leaders of activities such as All-School Assemblies. From a kindergartner who had never before attended school to a 5th-grade student who recently emigrated from China, all types of students need to be given equal opportunities to participate, and it is crucial to consider how diverse forms of participation count. Connecting with the broader community, Dewey built long-term partnerships with organizations, universities, and democratic school groups to sustain its vision of civic engagement for young people.

Exploring the role of leadership, this book has examined the tension between keeping a clear vision of civic engagement and valuing the processes of democratic collaboration. We saw a spectrum of relationships between vision and teacher voice, from teachers opting in and constructing the vision of the Schoolyard project to the mandatory participation of all students in All-School Assemblies. Within the initiatives discussed in this book, the theme of variability of implementation has persisted. When a school adopts a vision of civic engagement, it does not change the fact that teachers will have a wide range of reactions to this proposed goal. For school leaders, it is clearly important to acknowledge the variability of implementation in a schoolwide vision of civic engagement and to offer specific strategies that may meet teachers where they are in their learning processes about civic engagement.

LOOKING AHEAD

Democratic schools, like democracy itself, do not happen by chance. They result from explicit attempts by educators to put in place arrangements and opportunities that will bring democracy to life (Apple & Beane, 1995). Historically, the United States is rooted in a tradition of action, and its system of public school was founded on a democratic and civic mission (Carnegie Corporation of New York & CIRCLE, 2003). Because there are few examples of elementary school civic engagement (Hahn, 1998), it is imperative to offer cases of children participating in meaningful ways, and to show how adults foster their authentic and meaningful engagement.

In a climate that pushes schools to obey, master facts, and compete, we hope this book shows how schools can be powerful and proactive institutions. Even when the work might not be enough to transform injustices into justices, schools can be sites of engaged communities that inquire and assume agency. We hope this book will encourage greater university and community partnerships with public schools to foster and re-create education at its fullest.

Though the injustices to public schools under the mandates of high-stakes testing can still improve, this work shows that the curriculum does not have to be oppressively boring and irrelevant. It can be full of relevance, action, and engagement for the entire community. It can inspire young people to become civic agents and foster the belief that they can make a difference in their schools, communities, and the broader world.

Dewey Elementary provides one of the few examples in the literature of what civic engagement can look like in students' younger years. It helps us think expansively about the purpose of education, especially in a time of accountability. Dewey allows us to see civic engagement as a process of students and teachers collectively having agency and making a difference in their community. It shows that children can engage meaningfully in public schools and within a robust academic curriculum, especially when doing so is relevant to their worlds and motivated by empathy for the world and others in it. Dewey provides concrete examples of ways that schools from all backgrounds and experiences can seek to value the ability of young people to understand their world and become civic agents within it.

Methods

We established the relationship with Dewey when the principal read some of our work in a trade magazine (Mitra, 2008) and extended an invitation for us to visit her school to see ways in which student voice and civic engagement were happening in an elementary setting. Building out of that initial meeting, we explored ways in which we could study the civic engagement work happening at Dewey in a deeply contextual form of data collection. We chose to research Dewey using a longitudinal case study design model (Yin, 1994). Our work at Dewey spanned a 5-year time period.

Our research team consisted of two professors at Penn State (Dana Mitra and Stephanie Serriere) plus two research colleagues, 15 graduate students, and five undergraduate students. Mitra and Serriere trained the students in data collection techniques and hosted monthly meetings to discuss ongoing findings and data collection issues as they arose. As part of our broader data collection efforts at Dewey, members of our research team visited classrooms at least once a month and often much more frequently, depending on activities of interest happening in the classrooms.

Observations. In total, we conducted over 450-plus hours of observations. We conducted weekly observations of school events for the first 3 years, including Dewey's schoolwide assemblies and small school advisories. Over the 5 years, we also observed classrooms, faculty meetings, inservice trainings, and other critical events between students, teachers, administrators, and district staff, and recorded fieldnotes during our observations on laptop computers.

During all of the observations, researchers sat apart from the participants and did not involve themselves in the activities of the group. The intention of the observations was to capture the experiences of the cases to better illustrate the mechanisms and processes that fostered or hindered meaningful civic engagement, and specifically how leadership mattered. For particularly important observations, such as monthly Small School Advisories (SSAs), two research team members observed in tandem—one took fieldnotes on the big picture of the event; the other focused on capturing as many complete quotations of participants as possible. During observations, we also looked for supporting and refuting evidence of changes in students and teachers, as reflected in survey and interview data, described below.

Interviews. We conducted more than 50 interviews at the school during the 5 years, including focus group and individual interviews with students (21 interviews total), teachers (20 total), and administrators (8 interviews total). Semi-structured protocols during these interviews focused on the types of activities occurring and the types of outcomes for youth and the school that were emerging. Appendix B provides sample protocols. The teachers, administrators, and students featured in this book were each interviewed multiple times to examine changes over time and to use an iterative process to ensure saturation of data and validity of our analyses. Protocols continually were adapted as they were intended to capture responses to various ongoing initiatives.

Focus groups and interviews lasted at least 30 minutes each, and some conversations lasted much longer. They were recorded digitally and transcribed to capture the exact words of the interviewees. We also recorded notes from numerous informal conversations. We also administered an end-of-year short-response survey to the teachers on their goals and activities for their SSA groups during the 2nd year of data collection. We asked teachers their opinions of SSA groups, the activities they performed in the groups, and what they liked and didn't like about SSA activities. We coded these written responses by teachers in the same way that we did the spoken interviews.

Documents. We also gathered documents and artifacts. We collected students' own data including their comments, PowerPoints, and photos of students engaged in democratic practices through a range of activities. These documents included the Facebook group page created by 5th-grade teachers, emails to our team, emails to the staff from the principal, fieldnotes from a visit to the school by CNN regarding parental protest to mandated tests, one Dewey parent's public blog, an educational news podcast during which two Dewey teachers were interviewed, handouts given at faculty and parent meetings, and curricular resource materials.

Interactive Qualitative Analysis. As part of data collection and analysis for the contested spaces especially, we utilized a participatory methodology developed by Northcutt and McCoy (2004) called Interactive Qualitative Analysis (IQA). We conducted the IQA session in May 2012, near the end of 3 years of data collection. During the session, we sought to make sense of large amounts of data through listening and dialoguing with participants. The four key participants for the contested spaces chapter—Principal Shannon, Dewey principal; a parent of two students at Dewey; two Dewey teachers—met with our research team for approximately 2 hours for this IQA session. We decided to meet at the large conference table in Principal Shannon's office, as it was a private and regularly used space for all of the participants. We began by acknowledging (to the participants) broadly the "different things you have each done as advocates for a certain type of education" (IQA, May 16, 2012). Then we asked them to individually answer the question, "What are the supports that have allowed you to do this work?" We clarified and asked them to consider the people, places, and institutions from their past and present that have led them not only to their beliefs, but also to their actions, within the field of education. We gave each participant 3 x 5 cards (approximately five each) on which they were to write a word or phrase that came to mind in answer to our question. Then we invited each participant to place a card on the board and describe its significance. Each participant placed her card spatially on the board in relation to the others in order to suggest a possible *affinity*, or like phenomenon. The goal was to create the smallest number of affinities with the maximum richness of description. This method points to a high degree of trust among the participants and between our research team and the participants, as well as our hopes for a more grassroots and participatory analysis of our data.

Data analysis. All of these data were analyzed with a line-by-line analysis and open coding (Strauss & Corbin, 1990) to identify major inductive and deductive themes by using NVivo software. Semi-structured protocols during these interviews focused on the types of activities occurring and the types of outcomes for youth and the school that were emerging.

Special care was taken to search for discrepant evidence and claims that could be considered contradictory to the goals of the case activities. For example, we interviewed 5th-grade and younger students who were not participating in the Salad Girls initiative directly to gain their perspectives. We looked across the Salad Girls' experiences for differences in developmental outcomes as well as commonalities. We also shared quotations and drafts of this book with students, teachers, and administrators at Dewey as member checks of their own experiences. Our research team also searched for counterevidence to our claims in our NVivo data and during discussions at our research team meetings.

Sample Protocols

STUDENT FOCUS GROUP PROTOCOL

My name is _____ and I am from X University. I am here because I have
heard that you all participate in a Small School Advisory group. Is that true?
I want to learn all that I can about Small School Advisories. I don't know
anything about them, and I know you all are experts since you are in an SSA. I
want to thank you for meeting with me today. I hope that by the time we leave
today, I'll learn everything I can about SSAs so I can share that information
with other schools that might want to start their own SSA.
I want to remind you that your parent and/or guardian said it was okay for me
to interview you. This will take just a few minutes. If you do not want to be
interviewed, you can say so and no one will be upset. Is it okay if I interview you?
What happens in an SSA? What do you do in an SSA?
Why do you think we have SSAs in the first place? What are they for?
How did your SSA decide on this project?

- Where did the idea come from?
- How did you make a decision to do it?

What advice do you have for the teacher of an SSA? How should they act? What
should they do?

- What does your SSA leader do?
- What do you like about what he/she does?
- Any suggestions for your teacher? What would you like to see different?

What advice do you have for kids who might be in an SSA? How should they act?
What should they do?
What do you like best about SSA?
If you could change something about SSA, what would it be?
Are you involved in any service projects/community service here at school?
What is a community? What is community building?
What is your community? [examples—SSA, classroom, whole school,
neighborhood, other]
Is your SSA a community?
What is democracy? Is your SSA like a democracy?
Thank you for your important input.

STAFF FOCUS GROUP INTERVIEW PROTOCOL

Thank you for sharing your ideas with us about what's occurring at your school. I'd like to ask you some questions. *Your answers will remain anonymous and confidential.*

1. Perceptions of SSA
   a. What do you see as the purpose of the SSA?
   b. What do you hope *your students* gain or learn in your group? What do you hope *you* gain or learn?
   c. What sort of experiences do you hope students have?
   d. How has this project changed the climate of the school for you? Other faculty?
2. SSA activities
   a. What have you done so far in your SSA? [We've heard some groups have done some service learning; have any of you?]
   b. How do you decide what to do in your SSA?
   c. What are the successes that you have experienced in your SSA? Can you give me an example of a time in which you saw students gaining or learning something important?
   d. What are some struggles?
   e. How are the group interactions different from those in your classroom? How are they similar?
3. SSA process
   a. Do all kids participate in the SSA?
   b. What seems to determine how much they are involved in what you are doing?
   c. Would you say the small school groups are a place where students who aren't usually leaders get to be leaders, or is it a place where students who are already comfortable step up? Can you give an example? Is there a child in the group who has special needs, is just younger, or is disadvantaged in some way? Can you tell me about his or her participation in the group?
4. Service learning
   a. Are you involved in any service-learning projects?
   b. Do you see the SSA as relating to service-learning at all?
5. SSA group dynamics
   a. In your group, has there been a time when people had different ideas about what the group should do? Can you give me an example?
   b. Do you see them acting or interacting in new ways in this forum?
6. Perceptions of school
   a. What do you like about teaching at Dewey?
   b. What are the difficult parts of teaching here?

Thank you for your important input.

References

Abrams, D., & de Moura, G. R. (2002). The psychology of collective political protest. In Ottati, V., Tindale, R. S., Edwards, J., Bryant, F., Health, L., O'Connell, D., Suarez-Balzacar, Y. ,& Posavac, E. (Eds.), *The social psychology of politics* (pp. 193–214). New York, NY: Kluwer Academic..

Abu El-Haj, T. R. (2009). Becoming citizens in an era of globalization and transnational migration: Re-imagining citizenship as critical practice. *Theory into Practice, 48*(4), 274–282. doi: 10.1080/00405840903192714

Aitken, S. (2001). *Geographies of young people: The morally contested spaces of identity.* London, England: Routledge.

Angell, A. V. (2004). Making peace in elementary classrooms: A case for class meetings. *Theory & Research in Social Education, 32*(1), 98–104.

Apple, M. W., & Beane, J. A. (Eds.). (1995). *Democratic schools.* Alexandria, VA: Association for Supervision and Curriculum Development.

Apple, M. W., & Beane, J. A. (2007). Schooling for democracy. *Principal Leadership, 8*(2), 34–38.

Badiali, B. (2001). Self-assessment, program evaluation, and renewal. In J. E. Neapolitan (Ed.), *Taking stock of professional development schools: What's needed now* (pp. 444–462). New York, NY: Teachers College Press.

Badiali, B., & Titus, N. (2010). Co-teaching: Enhancing student learning through mentor-intern partnerships. *School-University Partnerships, 4*(2).

Badiali, B., Zembal-Saul, C., Dewitt, K., & Stoicovy, D. (2012). Shared inquiry: The professional development school as a laboratory of practice for preparing the next generation of teacher educators. In M. Macintyre Latta & S. Wunder (Eds.), *Placing practitioner knowledge at the center of teacher education: Rethinking the policies and practices of the education doctorate* (pp. 149–162). Charlotte, NC: Information Age Publishing.

Barton, K. C. (2008). Research on students' ideas about history. *Handbook of Research on Social Studies Education, 239.*

Battistich, V., & Horn, A. (1997). The relationship between students' sense of their school community and students' involvement in problem behavior. *American Journal of Public Health, 87,* 1997–2001.

Battistich, V., Solomon, D., Kim, D. I., Watson, M., & Schaps, E. (1995). Schools as communities, poverty levels of student populations, and students' attitudes, motives, and performance: A multilevel analysis. *American Educational Research Journal, 32*(3), 627–658.

Bauch, P. A., & Goldring, E. B. (1998). Parent-teacher participation in the context of school governance. *Peabody Journal of Education, 73*(1), 15–35.

Beck, T. A. (2005). Tools of deliberation: Exploring the complexity of learning to lead elementary civics discussions. *Theory & Research in Social Education, 33*(1), 103–119.

Belzer, A. (2005, Spring). Improving professional development systems: Recommendations from the Pennsylvania adult basic and literacy development system evaluation. *Adult Basic Education, 15*(1), 33–55.

Benford, R. D., & Snow, D. A. (2000). Framing processes and social movements: An overview and assessment. *Annual Review of Sociology,* 611–639.

Bickmore, K. (1999). Why discuss sexuality in elementary schools? In W. J. Letts IV & J. T. Sears (Eds.), *Queering elementary education: Advancing the dialogue about sexualities and schooling* (pp. 15–26). Lanham, MD: Rowman & Littlefield.

Biesta, G. (2007). Education and the democratic person: Towards a political conception of democratic education. *Teachers College Record, 109*(3), 740–769.

Billig, S. H. (2000). Research on K–12 school-based service-learning. *Phi Delta Kappan, 81*(9), 658–664.

Blase, J., & Blase, J. (2000). Effective instructional leadership: Teachers' perspectives on how principals promote teaching and learning in schools. *Journal of Educational Administration, 38*(2), 130–141.

Boyle-Baise, M., Hsu, M. C., Johnson, S., Serriere, S. C., & Stewart, D. (2008). Putting reading first: Teaching social studies in elementary classrooms. *Theory & Research in Social Education, 36*(3), 233–250.

Brezicha, K., Bergmark, U., & Mitra, D. (2015). One size does not fit all: Differentiating leadership to intentionally support teachers in school reform. *Education Administration Quarterly, 51*(1), 96–132.

Bronfenbrenner, U. (1994). Ecological models of human development. *Readings on the Development of Children, 2,* 37–43.

Brown, J. S., & Duguid, P. (2000). *Social life of information.* Boston, MA: Harvard Business School Press.

Bunting, E. (1991). *Fly away home.* New York, NY: Houghton Mifflin.

Burns, R. W., & Badiali, B. (2013). Preparing teacher educators in the professional development school context. In J. Perry & D. L. Carlson (Eds.), *In their own words: A journey to the stewardship of the practice in education* (pp. 41–58). Charlotte, NC: Information Age Publishing.

Cahill, C. (2007). The personal is political: Developing new subjectivities through participatory action research. *Gender, Place & Culture: A Journal of Feminist Geography, 14*(3), 267–292.

Camino, L. (2005). Pitfalls and promising practices of youth-adult partnerships: An evaluator's reflections. *Journal of Community Psychology, 33*(1), 75–85.

Camino, L., & Zeldin, S. (2002). From periphery to center: Pathways for youth civic engagement in the day-to-day life of communities. *Applied Developmental Science, 6*(4), 213–220.

Cammarota, J., & Fine, M. (Eds.). (2008). *Youth participatory action research in motion.* New York, NY: Routledge.

Carnegie Corporation of New York & CIRCLE. (2003). *The civic mission of schools.* New York, NY: Authors.

Center for Civic Education. (1996). Project Citizen. Denver, CO: National Conference of State Legislatures. Available at new.civiced.org/programs/project-citizen

Cervone, B. (2002, May). *Taking democracy in hand: Youth action for educational change in the San Francisco Bay area.* Providence, RI: What Kids Can Do with The Forum for Youth Investment.

Chinn, K. (1997). *Sam and the lucky money.* New York, NY: Lee & Low Books.

Coburn, C. E. (2003). Rethinking scale: Moving beyond numbers to deep and lasting change. *Educational Researcher, 32*(6), 3–12.

Coburn, C. E. (2004). Beyond decoupling: Rethinking the relationship between the institutional environment and the classroom. *Sociology of Education, 77,* 211–244.

Coburn, C. E. (2006). Framing the problem of reading instruction: Using frame analysis to uncover the micro processes of policy implementation. *American Educational Research Journal, 43*(3), 343–349.

Coburn, C. E., & Stein, M. K. (2006). Communities of practice theory and the role of teacher professional community in policy implementation. *New Directions in Education Policy Implementation: Confronting Complexity,* 25–46.

Cochran-Smith, M., & Lytle, S. (2006). Troubling images of teaching in No Child Left Behind. *Harvard Education Review, 76*(4), 668–697.

Cochran-Smith, M., & Villegas, A. M. (2015). Framing teacher preparation research: An overview of the field, Part 1. *Journal of Teacher Education, 66*(1), 7–20. doi: 10.1177/0022487711454907

Cohen, A., Vigoda, E., & Samorly, A. (2001). Analysis of the mediating effect of personal psychological variables on the relationship between socioeconomic status and political participation: A structural equations framework. *Political Psychology, 22*(4), 727–757.

Cohen, W. M., & Levinthal, D. A. (1990). Absorptive capacity: A new perspective on learning and innovation. *Administrative Science Quarterly,* 128–152.

Collatos, A. M., & Morrell, E. (2003). Apprenticing urban youth as critical researchers: Implications for increasing equity and access in diverse urban schools. In B. Rubin & E. Silva (Eds.), *Critical voices in school reform: Students living through change* (pp. 113–131). London, England: Routledge Farmer.

Cook-Sather, A. (2002). Authorizing students' perspectives: Toward trust, dialogue, and change in education. *Educational Researcher, 31*(4), 3–14.

Core Council of Governors. (2010). Common Core State Standards. Available at www.corestandards.org.

Counts, G. S. (1932). *Dare the schools build a new social order?* New York, NY: John Day Company.

Dalton, S., & Moir, E. (1996). Symbiotic support and program evaluation: Text and context for professional development of new bilingual teachers. In M. W. McLaughlin & I. Oberman (Eds.), *Teacher learning: New policies, new practices.* New York, NY: Teachers College Press.

Damon, W., & Phelps, E. (1989). Strategic uses of peer learning in children's education. In T. Berndt & G. Ladd (Eds.), *Peer relationships in child development* (pp. 135–157). New York, NY: John Wiley and Sons.

Daniels, D. H. K., Kalkman, D. L., & McCombs, B. L. (2001). Young children's perspectives on learning and teacher practices in different classroom contexts: Implications for motivation. *Early Education and Development, 12*(2), 253–273.

Darling-Hammond, L., & McLaughlin, M. W. (2011). Policies that support professional development in an era of reform. *Phi Delta Kappan, 92*(6), 81–92.

Davies, D. (2004). *Child development: A practitioner's guide.* New York, NY: Guilford Press.

Davis, O. L., Yeager, E. A., & Foster, S. J. (Eds.). (2001). *Historical empathy and perspective taking in the social studies.* New York, NY: Rowan & Littlefield.

Della Porta, D., & Diani, M. (1999). *Social movements: An introduction.* Malden, MA: Blackwell.

Denner, J., Meyer, B., & Bean, S. (2005). Young women's leadership alliance: Youth–adult partnerships in an all-female after-school program. *Journal of Community Psychology*, *33*(1), 87–100.

Developmental Studies Center. (1996). *Ways we want class to be: Class meetings that build commitment to kindness and learning.* Oakland, CA: Developmental Studies Center.

Dewey, J. (1909). *Moral principles in education.* Boston, MA: Houghton Mifflin.

Dewey, J. (1916). *Democracy and education.* New York, NY: The Macmillan Company.

Dewey, J. (1938/1998). *Experience and education.* West Lafayette, IN: Kappa Delta Pi.

Diceman, J. (2013). Dotmocracy. Available at dotmocracy.org

Dunn, A. W. (1916). *The social studies in secondary education.* Washington, DC: U.S. Government Printing Office.

Eccles, J., & Gootman, J. A. (2002). *Community programs to promote youth development.* Committee on Community-Level Programs for Youth. Board on Children, Youth, and Families, Commission on Behavioral and Social Sciences Education, National Research Council and Institute of Medicine. Washington, DC: National Academies of Science.

Einspruch, E. L., & Wunrow, J. J. (2002). Assessing youth/adult partnerships: The seven circles (ak) experience. *Journal of Drug Education, 32*(1), 1–12.

Eyler, J. (2002). Reflection: Linking service and learning—Linking students and communities. *Journal of Social Issues, 58*(3), 517–534.

Fielding, M. (2001). Students as radical agents of change. *Journal of Educational Change, 2*(2), 123–141.

Fielding, M. (2004). Transformative approaches to student voice: Theoretical underpinnings, recalcitrant realities. *British Educational Research Journal, 30*(2), 295–311.

Fisher, R. (2007). Dialogic teaching: Developing thinking and metacognition through philosophical discussion. *Early Child Development and Care, 177*(6–7), 615–631.

Fitchett, P. G., & Heafner. T. L. (2010). A national perspective on the effects of high-stakes testing and standardization on elementary social studies marginalization. *Theory and Research in Social Education, 38*(1), 298–316.

Flacks, M. (2007). "Label jars not people": How (not) to study youth civic engagement. In A. L. Best (Ed.), *Representing youth: Methodological issues in critical youth studies* (pp. 60–83). New York, NY, and London, England: New York University Press.

Flanagan, C. A. (2013). *Teenage citizens: The political theories of the young.* Cambridge, MA: Harvard University Press.

Flanagan, C. A., & Faison, N. (2001). *Youth civic development: Implications of research for social policy and programs.* Ann Arbor, MI: Society for Research in Child Development.

Fogarty, R., & Pete, B. (2007). Guide to adult learner. In R. J. Fogarty & B. M. Pete (Eds.), *From staff room to classroom: A guide for planning and coaching professional development* (pp. 14–36). Thousand Oaks, CA: Corwin Press.

Freire, P. (2000). *Pedagogy of the oppressed* (30th anniversary ed.). New York, NY: Continuum.

Fullan, M. G. (2001). *The new meaning of educational change* (3rd ed.). New York, NY: Teachers College Press.

Gahan, P., & Pekarek, A. (2013). Social movement theory, collective action frames and union theory: A critique and extension. *British Journal of Industrial Relations, 51*(4), 754–776. doi: 10.1111/j.1467-8543.2012.00912.x

Galloway, M., Pope, D., & Osberg, J. (2007). Stressed-out students-SOS: Youth perspectives on changing school climates. In D. Thiessen & A. Cook-Sather (Eds.), *International handbook of student experience in elementary and secondary school* (pp. 611–634). Dordrecht, The Netherlands: Springer.

Gambrell, L. B. (1985). Dialogue journals: Reading-writing interaction. *The Reading Teacher, 38*(6), 512–515.

Ginwright, S. (2005). On urban ground: Understanding African-American intergenerational partnerships in urban communities. *Journal of Community Psychology, 33*(1), 101–100.

Ginwright, S., Noguera, P., & Cammarota, J. (Eds.). (2006). *Beyond resistance! Youth activism and community change: New democratic possibilities for policy and practice for America's youth.* Oxford, England: Routledge.

Glickman, C. D., Gordon, S. P., & Ross-Gordon, J. M. (2004). *Supervision and instructional leadership: A developmental approach.* Boston, MA: Allyn and Bacon.

Graham, A., & Fitzgerald, R. (2010). Progressing children's participation: Exploring the potential of a dialogical turn. *Childhood, 17*(3), 343–359.

Greeno, J. G., & MMAP. (1998). The situativity of knowing, learning, and research. *The American Psychologist, 53,* 5–26. doi:10.1037/0003-066X.53.1.5

Hahn, C. L. (1998). *Becoming political: Comparative perspectives on citizenship education.* Albany, NY: State University of New York Press.

Halvorsen, A. L. (2009). Back to the future: The expanding communities curriculum in geography education. *The Social Studies, 100*(3), 115–120.

Harris, A., Wyn, J., & Younes, S. (2010). Beyond apathetic or activist youth: "Ordinary" young people and contemporary forms of participation. *Young: Nordic Journal of Youth Research, 18*(1), 9–32.

Hart, R. (1992). Ladder of participation, children's participation: From Tokenism to citizenship. *Innocenti Essays,* 4.

Harter, S. (1982). The perceived competence scale for children. *Child Development,* 87–97.

Haynes, J. (2008). *Children as philosophers: Learning through enquiry and dialogue in the primary classroom* (2nd ed.). New York, NY: Routledge.

Haynes, J., & Murris, K. (2011). *Picturebooks, pedagogy, and philosophy.* New York, NY: Routledge.

Henry, S. E., & Breyfogle, M. L. (2006). Toward a new framework of "server" and "served": De(and re)constructing reciprocity in service-learning pedagogy. *International Journal of Teaching and Learning in Higher Education, 18*(1), 27–35.

Hess, D. (2009). *Controversy in the classroom: The democratic power of discussion.* New York, NY: Routledge.

Hess, D., & McAvoy, P. (2014). *The political classroom: Evidence and ethics in democratic education.* New York, NY: Routledge.

Hoffman, M. L. (2001). *Empathy and moral development: Implications for caring and justice.* Cambridge, England: Cambridge University Press.

Honig, M. I., & Hatch, T. C. (2004). Crafting coherence: How schools strategically manage multiple, external demands. *Educational Researcher, 33*(8), 16–30.

Hoose, P., Hoose, H., & Tilley, D. (1998). *Hey, little ant.* Berkeley, CA: Tricycle Press.

Howard, R. W., Berkowitz, M. W., & Schaeffer, E. F. (2004). Politics of character education. *Educational Policy, 18*(1), 188–215.

Jacobs, P., Herrenkohl, L. R., & McCrohon, C. (1998). *Creating scientific communities in the elementary classroom.* Portsmouth, NH: Heinemann.

James, J. H., Kobe, J., & Zhao, X. (2014, November). The critical role of trust in facilitating mutualistic civic stances among young children. Paper presented at the annual meeting of Reconceptualizing Early Childhood Education, Kent, OH.

Jennings, L., & Mills H. (2009). Constructing a discourse of inquiry: Findings from a five-year ethnography at one elementary school. *Teachers College Record, 111*(7), 1583–1618.

Johnston, J. (2008). The citizen-consumer hybrid: Ideological tensions and the case of Whole Foods Market. *Theory and Society, 37*(3), 229–270.

Jubas, K. (2007). Conceptual con/fusion in democratic societies: Understandings and limitations of consumer-citizenship. *Journal of Consumer Culture, 7*(2), 231–254.

Kahne, J., & Westheimer, J. (1996). In service of what? The politics of service learning. *Phi Delta Kappan, 77*(9), 1–14.

Kahne, J., & Westheimer, J. (2006). The limits of political efficacy: Educating citizens for a democratic society. *PS: Political Science & Politics, 39*(2), 289–296.

Kawai, R., Serriere, S., & Mitra, D. (2014). Contested spaces of a "failing" elementary school. *Theory and Research in Social Education, 42*(4), 486–515.

Killen, M., & Smetana, J. (Eds.). (2014). *Handbook of moral development* (2nd ed.). New York, NY: Psychology Press.

Kirshner, B. (2004). *Democracy now: Activism and learning in urban youth organizations.* Palo Alto, CA: Stanford University.

Kirshner, B. (2008). Guided participation in three youth activism organizations: Facilitation, apprenticeship, and joint work. *Journal of the Learning Sciences, 17*(1), 60–101.

Kirshner, B., O'Donoghue, J., & McLaughlin, M. (2005). Youth adult research collaborations: Bringing youth voice to the research process. In R. Larson, J. Eccles, & J. Mahoney. (Eds.). *Organized activities as contexts of development: Extracurricular activities, after-school and community programs.* Mahwah, NJ: Lawrence Erlbaum Associates.

Kirshner, B., Pozzoboni, K., Jones, H. (2011). Learning how to manage bias: A case study in youth participatory action research. *Applied Developmental Science, 15*(3), 140–155.

Kohlberg, L. (1984). *Essays on moral development, volume 2. The psychology of moral development: The nature and validity of moral stages.* San Francisco, CA: Harper & Row.

Larson, R. W. (2000). Toward a psychology of positive youth development. *American Psychologist, 55*(1), 170–183.

Lave, J., & Wenger, E. (1991). *Situated learning: Legitimate peripheral participation.* New York, NY: Cambridge University Press.

Leithwood, K., & Poplin, M. S. (1992). The move toward transformational leadership. *Educational Leadership, 49*(5), 8–12.

Leonard, P. E., & Leonard, L. J. (2001). The collaborative prescription: Remedy or reverie? *International Journal of Leadership Education, 4*(4), 383–399.

Lerner, R. M., Lerner, J. V., Almerigi, J., Theokas, C., Phelps, E., Gestsdottir, S. Naudeau, S., Jelicic, H., Alberts, A. E., Ma, L., Smith, L. M., Bobek, D. L., Richman-Raphael, D., Simpson, I., Christiansen, E. D., & von Eye, A. (2005). Positive youth development, participation in community youth development programs, and community contributions of fifth grade adolescents: Findings from the first wave of the 4-H Study of Positive Youth Development. *Journal of Early Adolescence, 25*(1), 17–71.

Levinson, M. (2012). *No citizen left behind.* Cambridge, MA: Harvard University Press.

Lewison, M., Leland, C., & Harste, J. C. (2008). *Creating critical classrooms: K–8 reading and writing with an edge.* Mahwah, NJ: Lawrence Erlbaum Associates.

Lieberman, A. (1995). Practices that support teacher development: Transforming conceptions of professional learning. Innovating and evaluating science education. *NSF Evaluation Forums, 67*(1992–1994).

Lieberman, A., & McLaughlin, M. W. (1992). Networks for educational change: Powerful and problematic. *Phi Delta Kappan, 73*(9), 673. Available at search.proquest.com/docview/218465980?accountid =13158

Lieberman, A., & McLaughlin, M. (2000). Professional development in the United States: Policies and practices. *Prospects, 30*(2), 225–236.

Lindfors, J. W. (1999). *Children's inquiry: Using language to make sense of the world.* New York, NY: Teachers College Press.

Lipman, M. (2003). *Thinking in education* (2nd ed.). Cambridge, UK: Cambridge University Press.

Lipman, M., Sharp, A. M., & Oscanyan. F. S. (1980). *Philosophy in the classroom* (2nd ed.). Philadelphia, PA: Temple University Press.

Lobel, A. (1970). *Frog and toad are friends.* New York, NY: HarperCollins.

Louis, K. S, Marks, H. M., & Kruse, S. (1996). Teachers' professional community in restructuring schools. *American Educational Research Journal, 33*(4), 757–798.

Lundy, L. (2007). "Voice" is not enough: Conceptualizing Article 12 of the United Nations Convention on the Rights of the Child. *British Educational Research Journal, 33*(6), 927–942.

Matthews, G. (1992). *Dialogues with children.* Cambridge, MA: Harvard University Press.

Mayall, B. (1994a). Children in action at home and school. *Children's Childhoods: Observed and Experienced,* 114–127.

Mayall, B. (1994b). *Children's childhoods: Observed and experienced.* London, England: Falmer Press.

Mayall, B. (2000). Conversations with children: Working with generational issues. In P. Christensen & A. James (Eds.), *Research with children: Perspectives and practices* (pp. 120–135). London, England, & New York, NY: Falmer Press.

Mayes, E., Mitra, D., & Serriere, S. (2014). Figured worlds of citizenship. Paper presented at the College and University Faculty Assembly (CUAA) of the National Council for Social Studies. Boston, MA.

McIntyre, D., & Rudduck, J. (2007). *Improving learning through consulting pupil.* New York, NY: Routledge.

McLaughlin, M. W. (1993). Embedded identities: Enabling balance in urban contexts. In S. B. Heath & M. W. McLaughlin (Eds.), *Identity and inner-city youth* (pp. 36–68). New York, NY: Teachers College Press.

McLaughlin, M. W., & Mitra, D. (2001). Theory-based change and change-based theory: Going deeper, going broader. *Journal of Educational Change, 2*(4), 301–323.

McLaughlin, M. W., & Talbert, J. E. (2001). *High school teaching in context.* Chicago, IL: University of Chicago.

McQuillan, P .J. (2005). Pitfalls and possibilities: A comparative analysis of student empowerment. *American Educational Research Journal, 42*(4), 639–670.

Miller, L., & O'Shea, C. (1996). Partnership: Getting broader, getting deeper. In M. W. McLaughlin & I. Oberman (Eds.), *Teacher learning: New policies, new practices.* New York, NY: Teachers College Press.

Mills, C. W. (2000). *The sociological imagination.* Oxford, England: Oxford University Press.

Mirra, N., & Morrell, E. (2011). Teachers as civic agents toward a critical democratic theory of urban teacher development. *Journal of Teacher Education, 62*(4), 408–420.

Mitra, D. L. (2001). Opening the floodgates: Giving students a voice in school reform. *Forum, 43*(2), 91–94.

Mitra, D. L. (2003). Student voice in school reform: Reframing student-teacher relationships. *McGill Journal of Education, 38*(2), 289–304.

Mitra, D. L. (2004). The significance of students: Can increasing "student voice" in schools lead to gains in youth development? *Teachers College Record, 106*(4), 651–688.

Mitra, D. L. (2005). Adults advising youth: Leading while getting out of the way. *Educational Administration Quarterly, 41*(3), 520–553.

Mitra, D. L. (2007). The role of administrators in enabling youth-adult partnerships in schools. *NASSP Bulletin, 91*(3), 237–256.

Mitra, D. L. (2008). *Student voice in school reform: Building youth-adult partnerships that strengthen schools and empower youth.* Albany, NY: State University of New York Press.

Mitra, D. L. (2009a). Collaborating with students: Building youth-adult partnerships in schools. *American Journal of Education, 15*(3), 407–436.

Mitra, D. L. (2009b). The role of intermediary organizations in sustaining student voice initiatives. *Teachers College Record, 111*(7), 1834–1868.

Mitra, D., Mann, B., & Halvacik, M. (2013, April) Opting out: How states respond when parents object to statistical tests. Paper presented at the annual meeting of the American Educational Research Association, San Francisco.

Mitra, D. L., & Serriere, S. (2012). Student voice in elementary-school reform: Examining youth development in fifth graders. *American Educational Research Journal, 49,* 743–774. doi:10.3102/0002831212443079

Mitra, D. L., Serriere, S., & Stoicovy, D. (2012). The role of leaders in enabling student voice. *Management in Education, 26*(3), 104–112.

Mohr Lone, J. (2012). *The philosophical child.* Lanham, MD: Rowman & Littlefield.

Mol, A. (2009). Good taste: The embodied normativity of the consumer-citizen. *Journal of Cultural Economy, 2*(3), 269–283.

Muncey, D., & McQuillan, P. (1991). *Empowering nonentities: Students in educational reform.* Working paper #5. Providence, RI: School Ethnography Project, Coalition of Essential Schools, Brown University.

Mutz, D. (2002). The consequences of cross-cutting networks for political participation. *American Journal of Political Science, 46*(4), 838–855.

National Council for the Social Studies. (2013). *Social studies for the next generation: Purposes, practices, and implications of the college, career, and civic life (C3) framework for social studies state standards (Bulletin 113).* Silver Spring, MD: Author. Available at www.socialstudies.org/c3

National Governors Association (NGA) Center for Best Practices & Council of Chief State School Officers (CCSSO). (2014). Common Core State Standards Initiative. Available at www.corestandards.org.

Newhagen, J. E. (1994). Media use and political efficacy: The suburbanization of race and class. *Journal of the American Society for Information Science, 45*(6), 386–394.

Nolan, J., Badiali, B., Bauer, D., & McDonough, M. (2007). Creating and enhancing professional development school structures, resources and roles. In R. Bascom (Ed.), *Professional development schools: Enhancing teacher quality* (pp. 97–123). Philadelphia, PA: Research for Better Schools.

Northcutt, N., & McCoy, D. (2004). *Interactive qualitative analysis: A systems method for qualitative research.* Thousand Oaks, CA: Sage.

Nucci, L. (2001). *Education in the moral domain.* Cambridge, England: Cambridge University Press.

Nygreen, K., Ah Kwon, S., & Sánchez, P. (2006). Urban youth building community: Social change and participatory research in schools, homes, and community-based organizations. *Journal of Community Practice, 14*(1–2), 107–123.

Oakes, J., & Lipton, M. (2002). Struggling for educational equity in diverse communities: School reform as a social movement. *Journal of Educational Change, 3*(3–4), 383–406.

Ochoa-Becker, A. S., Morton, M. L., Autry, M. M., Johnstad, S., & Merrill, D. (2001). A search for decision making in three elementary classrooms: A pilot study. *Theory & Research in Social Education, 29*(2), 261–289.

Osler, A., & Starkey, H. (2005). *Changing citizenship: Democracy and inclusion in education.* London, England: Open University Press.

Pajares, F. (1997). Current directions in self-efficacy research. *Advances in Motivation and Achievement, 10*(149), 21–40.

Paley, V. G. (2009). *You can't say you can't play.* Cambridge, MA: Harvard University Press.

Palmer, P. (2007). *The courage to teach: Exploring the inner landscape of a teacher's life* (10th anniversary edition). San Francisco, CA: Jossey Bass.

Paris, D. (2012). Culturally sustaining pedagogy: A needed change in stance, terminology, and practice. *Educational Researcher, 41*(3), 93–97.

Parker, W. C. (2003). *Teaching democracy: Unity and diversity in public life.* New York, NY: Teachers College Press.

Parker, W. C. (2005). Teaching against idiocy. *Phi Delta Kappan, 86*(5), 344–351.

Parker, W. C. (2008). Knowing and doing in democratic citizenship education. *Handbook of Research in Social Studies Education,* 65–80.

Parker, W. C., & Hess, D. (2001). Teaching with and for discussion. *Teaching and Teacher Education, 17*(3), 273–289.

Perkins, D. F., & Borden, L. M. (2003). Risk factors, risk behaviors, and resiliency in adolescence. In R. M. Lerner, M. A. Easterbrooks, & J. Mistry (Eds.), *Handbook of psychology: Developmental psychology* (vol. 6., pp. 273–419). New York, NY: Wiley.

Piaget, J. (1951). *Play, dreams, and imitation in childhood.* London, England: Routledge.

Piaget, J. (1997). *The moral judgment of the child* (M. Gabain, trans.). New York, NY: Simon & Schuster.

Plato. (1970). *Laws* (T. Saunders, trans.). New York, NY: Penguin Books.

Ponder, J., & Lewis-Ferrell, G. (2009). The butterfly effect: The impact of citizenship education. *The Social Studies, 100*(3), 129–135.

Pope, A., Stolte, L., & Cohen, A. K. (2011). Closing the civic engagement gap: The potential of action civics. *Social Education, 75*(5), 267–270.

Pykett, J., Saward, M., & Schaefer, A. (2010). Framing the good citizen. *The British Journal of Politics & International Relations, 12*(4), 523–538.

Rock, T. C., Passe, J., Oldendorf, S., O'Connor, K., Heafner, T., Good, A., & Byrd, S. (2006). One state closer to a national crisis: A report on elementary social studies education in North Carolina schools. *Theory & Research in Social Education, 34*(4), 455–483.

Roeser, R. W., Midgley, C., & Urdan, T. C. (1996). Perceptions of the school psychological environment and early adolescents' psychological and behavioral functioning in school: The mediating role of goals and belonging. *Journal of Educational Psychology, 88*(3), 408–422.

Rogoff, B. (1990). *Apprenticeship in thinking: Cognitive development in social context.* New York, NY: Oxford University Press.

Ross, E. W. (Ed.). (1997). *The social studies curriculum: Purposes, problems, and possibilities.* Albany, NY: SUNY Press.

Rubin, B. (2012) *Making citizens: Transforming civic learning for diverse social studies class-rooms.* New York, NY: Routledge.

Rubin, B. C., & Jones, M. (2007). Student action research: Reaping the benefits for students and school leaders. *NASSP Bulletin, 91*(4), 363–378.

Ruble, D. N., Martin, C. L., & Berenbaum, S. A. (1998). *Gender development. Handbook of child psychology.* New York, NY: Wiley.

Rudduck, J. (2007). Student voice, student engagement, and school reform. In D. Thiessen & A. Cook-Sather (Eds.), *International handbook of student experience in elementary and secondary school* (pp. 587–610). Dordrecht, The Netherlands: Springer.

Sanders, F., Movit, M., Mitra, D., & Perkins, D. F. (2007). Examining ways in which youth conferences can spell out gains in positive youth development. *LEARNing Landscapes, 1*(1), 49–78.

Schultz, B. D. (2008). *Spectacular things happen along the way: Lessons from an urban class-room.* New York, NY: Teachers College Press.

Senge, P. M., & Scharmer, C. O. (2008). Community action research: Learning as a commu-nity of practitioners, consultants and researchers. In P. Reason & H. Bardbury (Eds.), *Handbook of Action Research* (pp. 195–207). London, England: Sage Publications.

Sergiovanni, T. J., & Starratt, R. J. (1998). *Supervision: A redefinition* (6th ed.). New York, NY: McGraw-Hill Higher Education.

Serriere, S. C. (2010). Carpet-time democracy: Digital photography and social conscious-ness in the early childhood classroom. *The Social Studies, 101*(2), 60–68.

Serriere, S. C. (2014). The role of the elementary teacher in fostering civic efficacy. *The Social Studies, 105*(1), 45–56.

Serriere, S. C., McGarry, L., Fuentes, D., & Mitra, D. (2012). How service-learning can ignite thinking. *Social Studies and the Young Learner, 24*(4), 6–10.

Serriere, S. C., Mitra, D. L., & Reed, K. (2011). Student voice in the elementary years: Fos-tering youth-adult partnerships in elementary service-learning. *Theory and Research in Social Education, 39*(4), 541–575.

Sherrod, L. R., Torney-Purta, J., & Flanagan, C. (Eds.). (2010). *Handbook of research on civic engagement in youth.* Hoboken, NJ: John Wiley and Sons.

Smith, F., & Barker, J. (2000). Contested spaces: Children's experiences of out of school care in England and Wales. *Childhood, 7*(3), 315. Available at search.ebscohost.com/login. aspx?direct=true&db=a9h&AN=5434933&site=ehost-live

Spillane, J. P., Halverson, R., & Diamond, J. B. (2001). Investigating school leadership prac-tice: A distributed perspective. *Educational Researcher, 30*(3), 23–28.

Stanley, W. B., & Nelson, J. L. (1994). The foundations of social education in historical con-text. In R. A. Martusewicz & W. M. Reynolds (Eds.), *Inside/out: Contemporary critical perspectives in education* (pp. 266–284). New York, NY: Routledge.

Strauss, A., & Corbin, J. (1990). *Basics of qualitative research: Grounded theory procedures and techniques.* Thousand Oaks, CA: Sage.

Talbert, J. E., & McLaughlin, M. (1994). Teacher professionalism in local school contexts. *American Journal of Education, 102,* 123–153.

TED. (2012). How to use a paper towel. Available at www.ted.com/talks/joe_smith_how_to_use_a_paper_towel?language=en

Torney-Purta, J., & Lopez, S. V. (2006). *Developing citizenship competencies from kindergar-ten through grade 12: A background paper for policymakers and educators.* Boulder, CO: Education Commission of the States: National Center for Learning and Citizenship.

United Nations. (1989). *Convention on the rights of the child.* Geneva, Switzerland: United Nations.

VanFossen, P. J. (2005). "Reading and math take so much of the time . . .": An overview of social studies instruction in elementary classrooms in Indiana. *Theory and Research in Social Education, 33*(3), 376–403.

Vygotsky, L. S. (1978). *Mind and society: The development of higher mental processes.* Cambridge, MA: Harvard University Press.

Wade, R. (2008). Service learning. In L. S. Levstik & C. A. Tyson (Eds.), *Handbook of research in social studies education* (pp. 109–123). New York, NY: Routledge.

Wartenberg, T. (2013). *A sneetch is a sneetch and other philosophical discoveries: Finding wisdom in children's literature.* Malden, MA: Wiley-Blackwell.

Watts, R. J., & Flanagan, C. (2007). Pushing the envelope on civic action: A developmental and liberation psychology perspective. *The Journal of Community Psychology, 35,* 779–792.

Wenger, E. (1998). *Communities of practice: Learning, meaning, and identity.* Cambridge, England: Cambridge University Press.

Westheimer, J., & Kahne, J. (2004). What kind of citizen? The politics of educating for democracy. *American Educational Research Journal, 41*(2), 237–269.

Wilbur, S. (2011). We the people (constitution song). Online video clip. YouTube. 11 Sep. 2011. Accessed 2 Nov. 2013. Available at www.youtube.com/watch?v=PIf7uFAKkJc&feature =related

Yin, R. K. (1994). *Case study research: Designs and methods* (2nd ed., vol. 5). Thousand Oaks, CA: Sage.

Yonezawa, S., & Jones, M. (2007). Using students' voices to inform and evaluate secondary school reform. In D. Thiessen & A. Cook-Sather (Eds.), *International handbook of student experience in elementary and secondary school* (pp. 681–710). Dordrecht, The Netherlands: Springer.

Youniss, J., & Hart, D. (2005). Intersection of social institutions with civic development. *New Directions for Child and Adolescent Development, 109,* 73–81.

Zeldin, S. (2004). Youth as agents of adult and community development: Mapping the processes and outcomes of youth engaged in organizational governance. *Applied Developmental Science, 8*(2), 75–90.

Zeldin, S., Camino, L., Calvert, M., & Ivey, D. (2002). *Youth-adult partnerships and positive youth development: Some lessons learned from research and practice in Wisconsin.* Madison, WI: University of Wisconsin-Extension.

Zeldin, S., Camino, L., & Mook, C. (2005). The adoption of innovation in youth organizations: Creating the conditions for youth-adult partnerships. *Journal of Community Psychology, 33*(1), 121–135.

Zukin, C., Keeter, S., Andolina, M., Jenkins, K., & Carpini, M. X. D. (2006). *A new engagement? Political participation, civic life, and the changing American citizen.* New York, NY: Oxford University.

Index

About the Authors

Dana L. Mitra is associate professor in the Department of Education Policy Studies at The Pennsylvania State University. Dana draws upon her previous experiences working in the education policy arena and the classroom to study civic engagement and student voice. Her research has included numerous projects that examine the intersection between the experiences of young people and the possibilities for their agency and participation in school decisionmaking, educational policy, and their communities.

Stephanie C. Serriere is an associate professor of elementary social studies at the School of Education, Indiana University Purdue University—Columbus. She serves as an affiliate faculty member in the Department of Curriculum & Instruction at The Pennsylvania State University. Stephanie brings a perspective from her experiences as a former elementary school teacher and instructor of elementary social studies methods, as well as working with schools on civic education practices. Her scholarship and work with schools supports teachers and schools in primary- and elementary-aged civic participation.

Michael D. Burroughs is acting associate director of the Rock Ethics Institute and senior lecturer of philosophy at The Pennsylvania State University. He also serves as an affiliate faculty member in the Penn State College of Education. For over a decade, Michael has practiced philosophical fieldwork with populations beyond the academy, facilitating philosophy discussion groups with and programming for children in K–12 schools, the elderly, and the incarcerated. He is the author of numerous book chapters and articles and is currently working on a co-authored book on philosophy with children (with Jana Mohr Lone) entitled The Perspectives of Children: Dialogue and Reflection in Schools (forthcoming).

Roi Kawai is an assistant professor in urban and multicultural education at University of Wisconsin's School of Education in La Crosse, Wisconsin. A former middle school literacy, math, and social studies teacher, Roi has taught elementary methods and social foundations of education courses. His research focuses on narratives of power and schooling of urban Black and Latino adolescents.

Eve Mayes is a doctoral student in the Faculty of Education and Social Work at the University of Sydney, Australia. As an English and English as a Second Language teacher, she engaged in teacher co-research as part of the University of Western Sydney's Teachers for a Fair Go research that propelled further collaborative research with high school students. Her research interests include social justice in education, student voice, collaborative/participatory research and writing, affective, negotiated, and creative curricula and pedagogies, and emerging forms of youth political engagement.